Effective Discipline Policies

How to Create a System that Supports
Young Children's Social-Emotional Competence

Sascha Longstreth, PhD
and Sarah Garrity, EdD

Gryphon House

www.gryphonhouse.com

Published by Gryphon House, Inc.

P. O. Box 10, Lewisville, NC 27023
800.638.0928; 877.638.7576 (fax)
www.gryphonhouse.com

Library of Congress Cataloging-in-Publication Data

Names: Longstreth, Sascha, author. | Garrity, Sarah, author.
Title: Effective discipline policies : how to create a system that supports
    young children's social-emotional competence / by Sascha Longstreth and
    Sarah Garrity.
Description: Lewisville, NC : Gryphon House, Inc., 2018. | Includes
    bibliographical references and index.
Identifiers: LCCN 2017045147 | ISBN 9780876597507 (pbk.)
Subjects: LCSH: School discipline. | Behavior modification. | Emotions in
    children. | Social skills in children. | Early childhood
    education--Psychological aspects.
Classification: LCC LB3012 .L66 2018 | DDC 371.5--dc23 LC record available at
    https://lccn.loc.gov/2017045147

Bulk Purchase

Gryphon House books are available for special premiums and sales promotions as well as for fund-raising use. Special editions or book excerpts also can be created to specifications. For details, call 800.638.0928.

Disclaimer

Gryphon House, Inc., cannot be held responsible for damage, mishap, or injury incurred during the use of or because of activities in this book. Appropriate and reasonable caution and adult supervision of children involved in activities and corresponding to the age and capability of each child involved are recommended at all times. Do not leave children unattended at any time. Observe safety and caution at all times.

Acknowledgments

From Sascha:

Thank you to my writing partner, Sarah, who has been a constant source of inspiration and joy throughout the writing journey. My family, especially Chris, Ethan, and Olivia, motivate me every day to become a better version of myself. I thank them for their ongoing love and support. Finally, I wish to thank all of the students who live the words in this book each day, for their hope and resilience—this book is for you.

From Sarah:

I would first like to thank all of the children, families, teachers, administrators, and early intervention specialists I have worked with and learned from over the years and who inspired me to write this book. To my family, John, Kyle, and Miles, thanks for always thinking I can do anything, even if it sounds crazy. Sascha, you are the other pea in my pod, the second half of my brain, and my third and fourth hand—we actually did this!

Table of Contents

Introduction

There is always one moment in childhood when the door opens and lets the future in.

—Deepak Chopra, author

What type of future do you imagine for the children in your early childhood program? Most of us who enter the field do so because we see the unlimited promise of childhood and have a real passion for helping children reach their full potential.

Unfortunately, however, caring for and educating young children is no easy task, especially when children exhibit challenging behaviors. During our many years in the field, we have seen children kick, hit, bite, spit, and engage in many other troubling behaviors. We have also seen passionate and talented teachers and administrators leave the field because of stress and burnout. Think for a moment about what the door to the future looks like in your early childhood program. Do some children walk confidently through the door, ready to take on the world? For other children, is the door so heavy that it appears to be made of steel? What does this door look like for families? for teachers? for you?

Caring for and educating young children in early childhood programs is rewarding yet difficult work, and we believe it is critical that systems are in place to support children, families, and staff to be their very best. Effective, high-quality behavior-guidance policies are one way to support both teaching and learning and to prevent and address challenging behaviors in early childhood settings. For the past ten years, we have been reviewing the research on effective behavior-guidance practices and have examined hundreds of behavior-guidance policies collected from early childhood programs across the United States. During this time, it has become clear

to us that programs need help developing high-quality behavior-guidance policies that reflect evidence-based practices. Effective behavior-guidance policies provide administrators with a blueprint that helps them build an infrastructure that supports the social, emotional, and academic success of all children. We believe that a systematic and intentional approach to behavior guidance can ensure that:

- evidence-based classroom practices for preventing and addressing challenging behaviors are consistently implemented across classrooms, resulting in a positive social-emotional climate and better child outcomes;

- relationships with families are meaningful, authentic, and strengths based;

- professional development is in line with program goals and best-practice recommendations; and

- decision making is fair and equitable.

Although there has been a great deal of research conducted on challenging behavior during the past twenty years, it is too time-consuming to sort through the evidence on best practices to figure out what is *essential* to include in a behavior-guidance policy. For this reason, we developed the Teaching and Guidance Policy Essentials Checklist (TAGPEC). The TAGPEC is an easy-to-use, thirty-item checklist that describes seven essential features of high-quality behavior-guidance policies for programs serving children from birth to eight years of age. We developed the

TAGPEC via an extensive review of the literature in the fields of general education, special education, early childhood education, early care and education, early childhood special education, educational administration, and school psychology and have refined it over the last several years through on our ongoing research project.

Overview of the Book

In chapter two, we present our philosophical approach to behavior guidance and discuss the five assumptions that are at the core of the TAGPEC. Because we feel so strongly about the critical importance of viewing children's culture and language as both strengths and teaching tools, chapter three describes how high-quality behavior-guidance policies can provide a blueprint for culturally relevant classroom practices and equitable decision making. Chapter four presents a research overview of the seven essential features of the TAGPEC, providing examples of how policy language can be crafted for each essential feature. In chapter six, we introduce a simple, five-step process for creating a high-quality behavior-guidance policy and, finally, in chapter seven, we hear from a pediatrician and a child psychiatrist team who explain the intricate connection between early childhood trauma and behavior.

A special introduction and some background information are needed regarding chapter seven, entitled "The Impact of Early Childhood Trauma on Children's Behavior and Adjustment." While we both feel as if we have the experience, academic training, and passion needed to guide programs to develop high-quality behavior-guidance policies that reflect the current research, our experience and training also tell us that there are some children who need intensive, comprehensive mental-health services that cannot always be provided in a typical early childhood setting. Because we felt so strongly about the need to address the reality and seriousness of early childhood trauma and the importance of early intervention in a book about challenging behavior, we asked our colleagues Dr. Pradeep Gidwani, a pediatrician, and Jeff Rowe, a clinical psychologist, to write our final chapter on trauma. If we are to build a true infrastructure of support for children, we must include everyone—teachers, administrators, program staff, families, early interventionists, and the early childhood mental-health community.

We hope that early childhood educators can use this book and the TAGPEC as a blueprint to help their program build an infrastructure that supports the social, emotional, and academic success of all children by providing guidance on how policy can be used to prevent and address challenging behaviors in the early years. Children do not walk through the door to the future on their own—they rely on dedicated, knowledgeable, and passionate educators who work together to teach children the skills they need to become successful, happy, and productive adults.

A Call to Action:

The Need for Effective, High-Quality Behavior-Guidance Policies in Early Childhood Settings

Over the past three years, Ms. Marina has taught four-year-olds. This is her first year teaching in a three-year-old classroom. As in the past, she developed classroom expectations and posted them on the wall. She reviews the rules each morning during circle time, during transitions, and when one or more of the children are having a hard time following the expectations. Although most of the children are following the rules, Zaryn is having difficulty. He constantly interrupts during circle and small-group time to share personal stories and questions, and he has a difficult time with the classroom expectations of sharing and taking turns. He speaks out of turn so often that the other children are left feeling frustrated.

During the past two weeks, Zaryn has begun pinching the other children during circle time. This afternoon, the director told Ms. Marina that the classroom parents are beginning to complain. Ms. Marina would like to help Zaryn learn how to better share and take turns so that other children have a turn to participate, but he seems to need extra time to do this. Ms. Marina feels torn between caring for the needs of all the children and taking the extra time to help Zaryn.

Unfortunately, scenarios such as these can be quite common in early childhood classrooms. During our years working as teachers, administrators, consultants, coaches, and higher-education faculty, we have experienced the stress, chaos, and emotions that result from children's challenging behavior. Many of the vignettes in this book come from our personal experiences working in the field. The vignette above, for example, comes from Sascha's experience working as a behavior consultant in an early childhood program. Challenging behavior is no fun for anyone, and the fact that you are reading this book right now means you are interested in learning more about how to prevent and address challenging behavior in early childhood settings.

Challenging behavior has been defined as "any repeated pattern of behavior that interferes with children's engagement in social interactions and learning and may include physical and verbal aggressions, prolonged tantrums, property destruction, self-injury, noncompliance, disruptive vocal and motor behavior, and withdrawal" (Powell, Fixsen, and Dunlap, 2003). Importantly, challenging behavior in the early years impedes learning, puts a child at high risk for later school failure, and is one of the strongest predictors of more serious problem behaviors in adolescence and adulthood, including mental health problems, delinquency, and engagement in criminal and violent activities (NRC and IOM, 2009). Not surprisingly, children's challenging behaviors are often listed as the number one concern of early childhood teachers and can lead to burnout, stress, and skilled and passionate teachers leaving the field. Administrators and families are also affected by children's challenging behavior. Recently, Sarah was in a community meeting and a principal looked at his phone, turned to her, and said, "Sorry, I have to leave. We have a child in one of our kindergarten classrooms who has been biting the other children, and the parent is waiting to speak to me." Sarah wondered, "Is he meeting the parent of the child who is biting or a parent of a child who has been bitten?" Both scenarios are possible and reflect just one of the many challenges faced by teachers, administrators, and families when dealing with challenging behaviors.

Recently, troubling data on preschool suspension and expulsion rates, as well as data indicating that young boys of color and young children with disabilities are suspended and expelled for behavioral challenges three to four times as often as other children (Office of Civil Rights, 2014), has received a great deal of national attention and has served as a wake-up call to the early childhood community. It is important to note that we define early childhood programs as those serving children from birth to age eight in a variety of settings—infant-toddler programs, public preschool programs including state preschool and Head Start, family child care homes, K–3 classrooms, campus child care centers, and private and for-profit early childhood education (ECE) programs. The National Association for the Education of Young Children (NAEYC) defines early childhood programs as those serving children from birth to age eight, and there is a growing interest in how children and families can be served by programming that reflects this age range.

The period of birth to eight years is unique in that it is a time of rapid development during which children learn many of the skills needed be successful in school, the workplace, and life. The development of self-regulation, the use of increasingly complex language, and the ability to think critically to both ask and solve problems are all hallmarks of this developmental period. Moreover, the development of the skills needed to make and keep friends, a positive self-identity and

self-esteem, and a strong sense of oneself as a learner all have their roots in early childhood. For these reasons, it is critical that adults support young children to become the very best they can be and that systems are in place to support teachers, administrators, and families as they go about this very important task. Fortunately, a great deal of information, based on years of research, is available that identifies practices and strategies shown to prevent and address challenging behaviors in young children. Unfortunately, however, these strategies are not being implemented on a consistent basis, as evidenced by the prevalence of challenging behavior, high rates of suspension and expulsion, and the identification of a "discipline gap" that calls attention to the troubling racial disparities in suspension and expulsion rates of children of color and those with disabilities. **Clearly, what we are doing is not working.** So what can be done? What steps can program leaders take to ensure that practices known to prevent and address challenging behavior are implemented in early childhood classrooms?

Effective, High-Quality Behavior-Guidance Policies

We propose that the use of high-quality behavior-guidance policies can help administrators ensure that *all* children learn the social and emotional skills needed to be successful. To be considered "high-quality," guidance policies first need to promote practices that are developmentally and culturally appropriate and, second, need be grounded in research on evidence-based practices. While this definition may seem simple at first, we believe that it is too broad for administrators to use when designing a guidance policy. For example, what exactly is meant by *developmentally and culturally appropriate?* How can administrators translate this into policy? There has been a great deal of research conducted on challenging behavior in the early years,

and we believe that it is too time-consuming for administrators to sort through the evidence on best practices to figure out what is essential for a program guidance policy. Moreover, the information available is not always based on the research and/or may provide conflicting recommendations based on ideology and/or personal experience and beliefs rather than evidence. (Consider, for example, the practice of time-out, which is a hotly debated topic in the literature). Clearly, given the troubling data on preschool suspension and expulsion and the lack of clarity as to what represents best practices, more support is needed to help administrators develop and implement effective policies that address challenging behavior.

The purpose of this book is to meet this need by providing clear, evidence-based information to early childhood program administrators about how to develop and implement high-quality behavior-guidance policies that support teaching and learning and prevent and address challenging behaviors. Since 2006, we have been reviewing the literature on effective behavior-guidance practices and have examined almost 400 behavior-guidance policies collected from early childhood programs across the United States. In this book, we share what we have learned to support early childhood administrators and program leaders in developing effective behavior-guidance policies that will help create and sustain a positive social-emotional climate and support the social, emotional, and academic success of all students.

Before we begin, however, it is important to note that we intentionally use the term *behavior-guidance policy* rather than discipline policy throughout this book; this distinction is key to our philosophical approach. While the Latin root of the word "discipline" means *discipulus* or pupil, its meaning has evolved over the years to be synonymous with punishment. Rather than trying to prevent challenging behaviors from occurring, many discipline policies focus on what will happen *after* the challenging behavior has already

occurred. In contrast, behavior guidance is preventative and refers to the practice of teaching children social-emotional skills such as self-regulation, cooperation, empathy, and responsibility. In this way, both prevention and teaching are central to the definition of behavior guidance. We believe that high-quality behavior-guidance policies can help early childhood program leaders ensure that:

- evidence-based classroom practices for preventing and addressing challenging behaviors are consistently implemented across classrooms, resulting in a positive social emotional climate and better child outcomes;

- relationships with families are meaningful, authentic, and strengths based;

- professional development is in line with program goals and best-practice recommendations; and

- decision making is fair and equitable.

In the following sections, we present information on why having a high-quality behavior-guidance policy is critical to the development of systems and practices that support teachers, administrators, and families as they seek to prevent and address challenging behaviors in early childhood settings.

Behavior-Guidance Policies: A Blueprint for Action

One way that we have come to think about the role of guidance policies in early childhood programs is to imagine them as a blueprint. Much as a blueprint provides an architect with the plans for a building, a guidance policy provides an administrator with a plan for creating an infrastructure that supports the social, emotional, and academic success of all children. Throughout this book, we use the term *infrastructure* to describe the organizational structure needed for the

effective operation of a center or school and to highlight the importance of a systematic approach to behavior guidance.

There are several compelling reasons why we have elected to focus our effort at the policy, or systems, level. Policies are an inherent component of effective and systemic service delivery and represent an intentional set of guiding principles designed to help translate the goals of the system into practice. In this way, policies provide a blueprint that guides program leaders as they work with their teams to build an infrastructure of support that is necessary if they are to implement practices in line with their mission. Think for a minute about the mission of your program. Does it involve teaching, learning, and supporting children's success? How do your current behavior-guidance policies support your mission? As leaders, administrators are responsible for ensuring that program policies and practices are in line with the mission of the program. Do your policies help or hinder all children to walk through the door to a future that is full of possibility and in which they will reach their full potential?

Current Context of Early Childhood Education

A systems-level approach to behavior guidance is especially important given the current context of ECE in the United States. Early childhood programs represent a hodge-podge of programs—for-profit, nonprofit, faith-based, Head Start, state preschool, co-ops, and family child care homes—many of which have disparate and often commingled, braided, or layered funding streams and programmatic requirements. In addition, universal preschool and transitional kindergarten initiatives mean that more and more preschool-aged children are being served on elementary school campuses. Kagan and colleagues (2007) have described ECE as a "nonsystem" because it lacks the overarching governance, funding, and accountability mechanisms present in the K–12 environment. This lack of infrastructure results in variability in the services provided to young children and their families in terms of quality, accountability, and equity. What this means for children is that some may be suspended or expelled for challenging behaviors while others are not, even if they exhibit the same behavior. In addition, while some programs may have a center, school, or district-wide discipline/guidance policy, in others, teachers, directors, or principals may develop their own policies based on their personal beliefs, experiences, and a real desire to make things better. Little guidance is provided by state licensing agencies, which most often provide information about what programs are prohibited from doing, such as corporal punishment, rather than what they should do to support social-emotional competence. In our reviews of program guidance policies, we have seen a tremendous amount of variability in terms of how challenging behaviors are addressed by program policy and the level of support provided to children, teachers, and families.

The Need for a Systems-Level Approach

Another reason we have decided to focus on policy is because research indicates that a systems-level approach to discipline that is understood by all stakeholders and is applied consistently reduces challenging behaviors and supports children, teachers, administrators, and families. In addition, implementing systems-level policies can be instrumental in helping to ensure that policies are evidence based. Here, we define *evidence based* as "a decision-making process that integrates the best available research evidence with family and professional wisdom and values" (Buysse, Wesley, and Winton, 2006). We have intentionally selected this definition as it reflects our belief that for behavior-guidance policies to be effective, they must take into consideration the local context and must recognize parents as an integral part of the decision-making process. Policies that incorporate evidence-based practices known to support young children's social and emotional competence in a systematic and intentional way can guide how administrators, teachers, and families address challenging behaviors and ensure that policies are enacted in ways that are equitable, fair, and support children's success. Like blueprints, policies are not only key in planning programs but are also a critical reference point when decisions need to be made. With a strong blueprint for success in hand, administrators can feel confident that they are taking action to prevent misbehavior from occurring and are addressing it appropriately and fairly when it does occur.

The key role of policy is highlighted by the Teaching Pyramid, a tiered model of support frequently used in early childhood settings to help programs promote social-emotional development and support children's appropriate behavior through the use of evidence-based strategies (Fox et al., 2003). At the base of this model (see Figure 1) are systems and policies that promote and sustain the use of evidence-based practices. In this way, policies are the foundation for the supportive services described at every level of the Teaching Pyramid, reflecting our belief that behavior-guidance policies provide the blueprint needed to build an infrastructure that supports children's social, emotional, and academic success.

Figure 1: The Teaching Pyramid

The Pyramid Model:

Promoting Social and Emotional Competence and Addressing Challenging Behavior

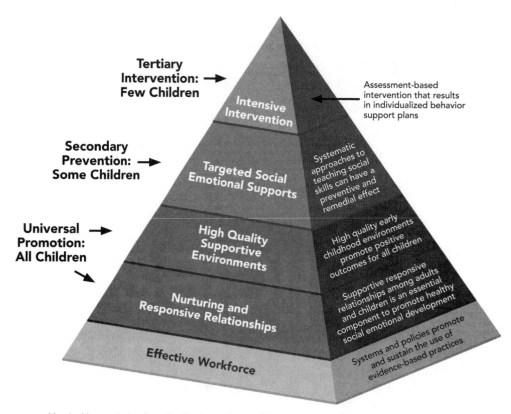

Used with permission from the Center on the Social and Emotional Foundations for Early Learning.

Recent Policy Initiatives

Another reason we have decided to focus our efforts at the policy level is that the important role of high-quality discipline/behavior guidance policies in preventing and addressing challenging behaviors has been highlighted by several recent policy initiatives and guidelines. A summary of these recommendations is found in Table 1.

Table 1: Recent Policy Recommendations

Author	Title	Statement Related to Policy and/or Suspension and Expulsion
US Department of Health and Human Services and the US Department Of Education	*Policy Statement on Expulsion and Suspension Policies in Early Childhood Settings*	A primary aim of this document is to provide recommendations to states and early childhood programs on how to establish "preventative disciplinary, suspension, and expulsion policies and administering those policies free of bias and discrimination."
US Department of Education	*Guiding Principles: A Resource Guide for Improving School Climate and Discipline*	"Schools that have discipline policies or codes of conduct with clear, appropriate, and consistently applied expectations and consequences will help students improve behavior, increase engagement, and boost achievement."
Child Care and Development Fund (CCDF)	*Child Care and Development Block Grant (CCDBG) Act of 2014*	States are required to provide information to families, the public, and child care providers on "policies regarding the social-emotional and behavioral health of young children, which may include policies on expulsion of preschool-aged children in early childhood programs receiving CCDF funding."
Office of Head Start	*Head Start Performance Standards*	Programs are required to "prohibit or severely limit" suspensions and "explicitly prohibit" expulsions. Programs are required to "engage a mental health consultant, collaborate with parents, and utilize appropriate community resources" in response to a child's challenging behavior.
National Association for the Education of Young Children (NAEYC)	*Standing Together Against Suspension and Expulsion in Early Childhood*	"We must . . . work together to create systems, policies, and practices that reduce disparities across race and gender, preventing and eventually eliminating expulsions and suspensions in early childhood settings."

Our hope is that administrators of early childhood programs can use this book to develop effective behavior-guidance policies that are in line with these policy recommendations.

Benefits to Children, Teachers, Families, Administrators, and the Community

Finally, and perhaps most importantly, we have decided to focus on policy because we believe that engaging in the process of writing and implementing high-quality behavior-guidance policies will benefit everyone involved. Rather than relying on piecemeal approaches to dealing with challenging behavior, a guidance policy provides all stakeholders with a blueprint for how to effectively respond to behavioral challenges and to create an infrastructure that supports the social, emotional, and academic success of all children. With a strong blueprint for success in hand, administrators can feel confident that they are taking action to *prevent* misbehavior from occurring and that they are addressing it appropriately and fairly when it does occur. Because of our belief in the importance of high-quality behavior-guidance policies, we developed the Teaching and Guidance Policy Essentials Checklist to support program leaders and their staff as they engage in the process of developing policies that reflect what research tells us is best for children, teachers, and families. This tool is described in the following section and is used throughout this book to guide you as you think about and develop effective, high-quality behavior-guidance policies.

The Teaching and Guidance Policy Essentials Checklist

As noted above, we developed the TAGPEC because of our belief that high-quality behavior-guidance policies are essential to supporting the social, emotional, and academic success of all children. The TAGPEC is an easy-to-use, thirty-item checklist that describes seven essential features of high-quality discipline policies for programs serving children from birth to eight years of age. The TAGPEC was developed via an extensive review of the literature in the fields of general education, special education, early childhood education, early care and education, early childhood special education, educational administration, and school psychology and has been refined over the last several years through our ongoing research project. Figure 2 illustrates how the TAGPEC and its seven essential features can be used to build an infrastructure that supports the social, emotional, and academic success of all children.

Figure 2: Seven Essential Features of TAGPEC

Social, Emotional, and Academic Success for All Children

EF 1   Intentional Focus on Teaching Social-Emotional Skills

EF 2   Developmentally and Culturally Appropriate Learning Environment

EF 3   Setting Behavioral Expectations

EF 4   Preventing and Addressing Challenging Behaviors Using a Tiered Model of Intervention

EF 5   Working with Families

EF 6   Staff Training and Professional Development

EF 7   Use of Data for Continuous Improvement

A Call to Action: The Need for Effective, High-Quality Behavior-Guidance Policies in Early Childhood Settings

CHAPTER TWO

2

A Humanistic Approach to Child Guidance

Mrs. K's transitional kindergarten class was seated on the rug listening to a recording of "The Three Billy Goats Gruff" when Robbie arrived to school with his father. Mrs. K, who was turning the pages of the book to go along with the tape recording, glanced briefly at Robbie and signaled for her assistant teacher to offer Robbie some breakfast. Robbie put his coat in his cubby and sat at the table to eat his breakfast. He finished his meal in silence and refused to join the circle when prompted by the assistant teacher. Instead, he remained at the table, with his arms crossed tightly across his chest and kicking the underside of the table every few minutes. As the book finished, Mrs. K asked the children to come up to the front of the circle and select the center where they would like to work. After all the children had made their selections, Mrs. K approached Robbie and said, "Well, Robbie, the only center that is still available is the science center. I guess you will have to go there because you chose not to join your friends at circle time."

As Robbie walked to the science center, he pushed Jamar, who was building with Legos at the Lego table, causing Jamar's structure to fall over. After comforting Jamar and helping him pick up the Lego pieces, Mrs. K walked over to the science center. When Robbie saw Mrs. K approach, he ripped a poster of the four seasons off the wall and pushed the scale off the table. "That's it, Robbie. This behavior is not okay. We don't hit our friends, and it is not okay to destroy property. You need to go to the quiet area and think about what you have done." Robbie glared at her, slowly walking to the quiet area, where he remained until his mother picked him up after receiving a call from the principal.

As described in chapter one, effectively addressing challenging behaviors such as Robbie's requires a systematic and intentional approach that is grounded in the belief that all children can be successful. In this chapter, we will present our philosophical approach to behavior guidance, highlighting five key assumptions that are essential if programs are to develop policies and practices that support the social, emotional, and academic success of all children. Throughout this chapter, we will use the vignette above to highlight each of these assumptions.

A Humanistic Approach to Behavior Guidance

- The role of the adult is to teach children appropriate social-emotional skills.

- Relationships guide and regulate behaviors.

- Behavior is communication.

- Each child is a unique individual.

- Implicit bias affects decision making.

In this book, we approach child guidance from a humanistic rather than a behavioral perspective. The term *humanistic* refers to viewing the child holistically, rather than only in terms of observable behaviors. Humanistic theories, introduced by psychologists such as Abraham Maslow and Carl Rogers in the mid-twentieth century, emphasize people's inherent ability to attain self-actualization—or their best self. The philosophical approach underlying the TAGPEC reflects a humanistic approach that values each child's personal worth, agency, and creativity as she strives to reach her individual potential. From this vantage point, the role of the adult is to assist children to reach their highest potential (Rogers, 1961) and to treat all children with dignity and respect. As such, our approach to teaching and guidance prohibits the use of strategies that are punitive, degrading, or dehumanizing. We believe that each child has the creative capacity and free will to work toward her best self. The first of our key assumptions, that it is the adult's role to teach children appropriate social-emotional skills, is described below.

The Role of the Adult Is to Teach Children Appropriate Social-Emotional Skills

Traditional approaches to discipline typically involve punishing children for misbehavior; valuing obedience rather than learning; and the use of strategies that may hurt, shame, or belittle children. Behavior guidance, on the other hand, focuses on teaching children socially accepted behavior. It involves identifying appropriate and inappropriate behaviors; teaching children effective strategies for expressing their emotions and solving their conflicts; and helping children to develop self-regulatory skills such as impulse control, empathy, and perspective-taking (Kaiser and Rasminsky, 2011). Importantly—and reflecting the TAGPEC's goal of creating an infrastructure that supports children's social, emotional, and academic success—child guidance is *preventative* rather than *reactive*. Rather than punishing a child after the behavior has occurred, a focus on prevention seeks to teach children the skills they need to be their best possible selves and to provide a classroom environment in which children can be successful.

Unfortunately, using punishment and rewards to "guide" children's behavior is very common in early childhood settings. Asking a child to move his card from yellow to purple, the use of time-out, and sticker charts are common strategies used to address challenging behavior in early childhood classrooms. Punishment, which stems from behaviorism, is meant to deliver an unpleasant response to the child's behavior in an attempt to weaken or extinguish it. In contrast, rewards are pleasant responses, such as stickers, green cards, or prize boxes, meant to increase children's positive behaviors. We can all think of times as adults when we have received punishments and rewards. Receiving a speeding ticket, for example, is a clear example of a punishment that is meant to decrease speeding behavior. A pay bonus received from work for extra effort is a reward. Although punishment and rewards have been shown to produce clear short-term results, they do not necessarily guide people toward producing the appropriate behavior. Does receiving a speeding ticket always result in one never speeding again? As soon as the punishment disappears, the behavior returns. Moreover, we want children to make good choices because they are the right things to do rather than because they will get a prize or reward.*

---

*Extrinsic rewards are appropriate for some children at the second or third tier of tiered models of intervention.

Let's reflect on the effectiveness of the teacher's approach in the vignette above. Keeping in mind that our ultimate goal is to teach children the skills needed to regulate their emotions and behavior in a social environment, we must ask ourselves the following:

- What has Robbie learned from this interaction with his teacher?

- Has he learned any skills that can help him self-regulate his behavior and act in a more socially acceptable way the next time something like this occurs?

- How has this interaction affected Robbie's perceptions about himself, his classmates, and his teachers?

- Has the teacher supported him to become his best possible self?

Let's now consider what our humanistic approach means for Robbie and Mrs. K. How could the teacher have responded in a more humanistic way? When Robbie arrived late, Mrs. K. might have noticed that he looked upset and wondered why his dad was bringing Robbie to school instead of his mom, which was the family's typical arrangement. Because she has learned to read Robbie's cues and notices that his behavior is escalating as he begins to kick the table, she asks her assistant teacher to help the other children select their centers for choice time, walks to the table, and gets down at Robbie's level. She says something that shows that she empathizes with and cares for him. For example, "Robbie, I am glad you are here today. It seems like you are feeling really frustrated and angry. Was it a hard morning?" This a comment sends a message that Robbie is being heard by his teacher and gives a name to what he is feeling— *frustrated*. By teaching Robbie that words can be used to describe complex feelings like frustration, Mrs. K. is modeling and teaching Robbie how to express emotions in a socially acceptable manner.

Once Mrs. K. has established a connection with Robbie and validates his feelings, she suggests a few choices for how Robbie might participate in center time. One of these choices includes taking a look at the new train puzzle that is in the block area, because she knows Robbie is fascinated by trains. It is important to note that this approach isn't rewarding or reinforcing Robbie's bad behavior, as some teachers and administrators fear; rather, Mrs. K. is individualizing her teaching practice to help Robbie successfully transition into the classroom routine after a difficult morning. While Mrs. K's strategy is designed to meet Robbie's individual need at that moment, it is part of her overall approach to behavior guidance, the goal of which is to intentionally teach children social and emotional skills throughout the day in multiple settings.

Now let's consider what might happen if, despite her efforts to connect with Robbie and guide him into center time, Robbie still knocks over Jamar's Lego structure on the way to the block area. Mrs. K would view this incident as an opportunity to teach rather than to punish. She might, for example, remind Robbie of the classroom rule to be kind and ask him to look closely at Jamar's sad (or angry) face and consider how Jamar is feeling. Hopefully, Mrs. K will have the knowledge and skills that allow her to draw upon a host of strategies that she can use in this situation, all of which support her goal of teaching Robbie the social and emotional skills he needs to be successful in her classroom. Unlike punishment, teaching children self-coping skills when they are feeling dysregulated provides them with alternative ways of behaving.

It takes more initial effort on the teacher's part to problem solve with the child when he is feeling distressed, but the results are long lasting as children learn to self-regulate their emotions and solve their own problems.

In sum, behaviorist practices such as punishment and rewards do not teach children what to do; they only tell them what *not* to do. So, when we exclude a child from activities by using time-out or sending the child to the quiet area without teaching him how to calm down and express his feelings in a more socially acceptable way, we are really only teaching that child that we are unavailable to help them regulate their intense, negative emotions and teach them a better way. Since many young children—especially those at risk because of poverty, trauma, or a variety of biological conditions—have not always learned how to self-regulate their behavior,

they will continue to act out until they learn more socially acceptable ways to communicate their feelings. The recognition that children need to be taught self-regulation and social-emotional skills reflects our contention that, to decrease challenging behavior in the early years, programs must develop systems and policies that support early childhood educators to teach children how to get their needs met in ways that not only work for the child but are also socially acceptable. When we do this, challenging behavior decreases because children learn that there is a better way to do things. Rather than punish children for their misbehavior, we need to show empathy and compassion, just as Mrs. K. does in the revised vignette. Relationships are the child's most important link to learning, and the importance of relationships is the second assumption of our humanistic approach to behavior guidance.

Relationships Guide and Regulate Behavior

Relationships are the foundation for teaching and learning in the early years, and positive relationships provide a powerful context for learning. When we view children's behavior from a humanistic lens, we don't see the problem behaviors as the foci; instead, we consider the child's behavior in context. The TAGPEC is grounded in the belief that child behavior is transactional in nature, with both the teacher and the child contributing to the relationship (Ciciolla, Crnic, and Gerstein, 2013). Because problem behaviors occur within the context of the teacher-child relationship, they are best resolved within these relationships via the socialization practices of the teachers. Central to this approach is that we don't isolate the problem behavior as being within the child; instead, we consider how the behavior results from the interplay of the child within his social world.

Research shows that children who have secure relationships with their early childhood teachers have positive peer relationships and good teacher relationships in elementary school. It also shows that children who have secure relationships with their teachers have less challenging behaviors and higher levels of social and emotional competence in school, both of which contribute to academic success. In contrast, children who have insecure relationships with teachers have more difficulty and conflict with peers and teachers as they move throughout the educational system. Consider for a moment your own personal development. Can you think of a favorite teacher or someone whom you consider a mentor? How did this person make you feel about yourself and your ability to be successful? Did this person teach you any hard lessons? What did this person do to help you reach your individual potential and be your very best self?

Our own personal development and ability to cope with life's stressors is grounded in consistent and caring relationships with people who know us well and respond in ways that are contingent and responsive. In the revised vignette, Mrs. K. reads Robbie's cues early on and notices that something is not right with him. Emotional cues and behavior are a children's language, especially when they are preverbal or still learning how to use language to communicate their thoughts and emotions. Even when children acquire more complex and abstract language, nonverbal cues provide a basis for communication. This is true for adults as well. Has there ever been a time when you told your spouse, partner, or friend that you were "fine," when your behavior and body language were sending a much different message?

Imagine for a moment a time when you felt frustrated, out of control, angry, and alone. Perhaps you woke up late, spilled your coffee in the car, and caught every red light on the way to work. You finally make it, only to have the other staff look at you with patronizing and irritated expressions. One staff member snaps, "Where have *you* been?" You feel taken aback and even more upset. Seeing your frustration, another staff member sharply tells you to "go and pull yourself together" so that you "can get to work like everyone else." How would this exchange make you feel? Most likely, it would leave you feeling even more angry and alone, and you may feel like you want to throw your coffee cup across the room (or even hit someone!).

Now, consider an alternate scenario. Imagine if, when you walked in late to work, a staff member instead says, "Hi, Sascha. You look like you had a difficult morning. I know how

that goes. You have parents here to meet you. Would it be helpful if I met with them for a few minutes first so that you can get settled?" Wow, what a different experience this would be! Rather than judging you for being late, your coworker read your cues and recognizes the underlying emotions being communicated through your behavior. The negative feelings you were experiencing wouldn't escalate and you wouldn't throw that coffee cup across the room! Instead, you would feel calmer, valued, and better able to face the day ahead. Receiving support when we feel vulnerable is what we hope for as adults and is critically important for children.

When children are feeling dysregulated, they need us to empathize with them before we redirect their behavior. In other words, they need to be heard and not judged.

> Receiving support whe[n] we feel vulnerable is what we hope for as adults and is critically important for children.

As we respond to children's needs in ways that are responsive and caring, we establish trust and an emotional connection, which in turn helps the child feel heard and understood. A teacher's ability to respond to children's negative emotional cues with sensitivity is a hallmark of a humanistic approach. This approach opens the door to a deeper and more secure relationship with the child. In the revised vignette, Mrs. K's actions allow Robbie to feel understood rather than judged for his feelings and behavior, as her response is deeply compassionate and sends the message that Robbie is valuable and worthy of being listened to. As our vignette shows, teachers build relationships through a variety of behaviors including using a calm tone of voice, affectionate behaviors, and contingent responses that let the child know that he is being listened to.

Not only do young children communicate their emotional states via both verbal and nonverbal cues, they are also adept at reading our emotional cues. Have you ever walked into a classroom and just "felt the love?" Conversely, have you ever entered a classroom where you could sense that no one, including or maybe especially, the teacher, wanted to be there? When you are feeling joyful, children sense it and respond with playful behaviors. When you are feeling tense or angry, they sense it and may respond with challenging behaviors. We can all think of a time when a child has responded to our own angry or sad cues with problem behaviors, and being aware of our role in children's challenging behavior is central to our humanistic approach. Essential Feature 6, Staff Training and Professional Development, and Essential Feature 7, Use of Data for Continuous Improvement, address how program policy can put systems in place to support teachers as they reflect on how their behavior and beliefs may contribute to the presence or absence of challenging behavior in the classroom. It is critical that both teachers and administrators become more aware of when they feel triggered by misbehavior so they can, in turn, regulate their own emotions before attending to those of the child.

Developing feelings of mutual respect is key to having a strong emotional connection with a child. When children feel respected and safe and when their needs are met, there is no longer a need for the child to use challenging behavior to communicate. As we learn to recognize and meet children's needs, we build deeper relationships with children characterized by our ability to be more emotionally available to their emotional cues and feelings. In this way, our efforts at teaching children must focus not just on their behaviors, but on the underlying reasons for their behaviors. As adults, it is our responsibility to learn more about what it is that is being communicated by children's challenging behavior and to understand that behavior is a form of communication.

Behavior Is Communication

If asked to describe challenging behavior in early childhood, what would you say? Hitting and kicking? Biting or throwing toys? Defiance? A major goal of this book is to help reframe your description of challenging behavior and encourage you to think of behavior as communication. What exactly does this mean?

A child's challenging behavior is a signal that something is not right. Behavior sends a message that children are tired, hungry, frightened, bored, sad, or angry—or a combination of any of these. Often, when they act out, children lack the skills to express their needs appropriately, or they are too dysregulated to use the skills they have. A child who does not feel safe, for example, may try to seek order and control by getting everything in the classroom to come to a complete stop by pushing over a cubby or throwing a chair. Or, a child who desperately wants the teacher's attention may learn that the most effective way to get this attention is by hitting another child. Sensory issues are another reason why children misbehave and are often overlooked as a cause of misbehavior. Children with sensory issues may seek out or avoid sensory experiences because they are seeking or avoiding physical sensations. They may punch things, bite and push other children, throw things, or, on the opposite end of the spectrum, avoid activities that involve certain textures such as grass, mud, string, and/or certain foods. More seriously, the behavior of some children is evidence of early childhood trauma, such as physical or sexual abuse, domestic violence, and/or neglect. Early childhood trauma can also be the result of war, accidents, or a natural disaster.

When children misbehave, we should always assume they are sending us a message. This message is often difficult for us to hear. Sometimes we have difficulty reading cues, and sometimes we are triggered by our own experiences and have a hard time coping with the challenging behaviors. Undoubtedly, children's misbehaviors can be confusing and frustrating; however, a humanistic approach to behavior guidance reminds us that is our responsibility to teach children how to express their emotions and get their needs met in more socially acceptable ways. The more children feel misunderstood, the more they intensify their behaviors. In the original vignette, Robbie's behavior escalates throughout the morning as his messages go unheeded and his needs continue to be ignored. Once we understand that behavior is communication, there are many steps we can take to determine the function of the behavior—what the child is trying to accomplish through his behavior. We must ask ourselves: "What need is the child trying to meet with this behavior? What is the child trying to tell us?" Uncovering the meaning, or function, of children's behavior is a key strategy used in tiered models of intervention called for in Es-

sential Feature 4, Preventing and Addressing Challenging Behaviors Using a Tiered Model of Intervention. Once we figure out what a child is trying to communicate or achieve by his or her behavior, we can then teach him more socially acceptable ways to get his needs met.

Let's consider Robbie's behavior from this functional perspective. What could be the purpose or function of Robbie's behavior? Examining the series of events that lead to Robbie being sent home helps us to understand the reason for his challenging behavior and what he is trying to communicate. Robbie is clearly upset and dysregulated when he arrives to school, as evidenced by his affect when he enters the room and his refusal to join circle time. Again, think of how you feel in the morning when your alarm doesn't go off, you spill your coffee, and you hit every red light on the way to work. Does it make sense that Robbie is feeling upset or angry? Perhaps he wants the teacher to notice and empathize with him. When the teacher doesn't read his cues, Robbie escalates his behavior and begins kicking the table, still receiving no response from the teacher. Many times the function of a child's behavior is to get the teacher's attention, whether it be positive or negative. Let's take another look at what happens when Mrs. K. does give Robbie her attention when it is time to select learning centers:

After all the children had made their selections, Mrs. K approached Robbie and said, "Well, Robbie, the only center that is still available is the science center. I guess you will have to go there because you chose not to join your friends at circle time."

Again, think of how you would feel if the first greeting you received upon arriving at work after a stressful morning was, "Well, nice of you to show up today. I hope you are ready to get to work." Recalling the transactional

nature of challenging behavior, Mrs. K. is clearly upset by Robbie's refusal to join circle time when asked, and her feelings affect her ability to respond to Robbie in a way that is empathetic and relationship based.

It is also important to consider the learning environment and curricular approach being used in the classroom. Mrs. K. lets Robbie know that he will have to go to the science center because it is the only center still available. Why is it that there are no children at the science table? Unfortunately, science is often the most boring center in an early childhood classroom, and being sent to the science table could be viewed as a form of punishment. (Mrs. K.'s word choice and tone seem to imply that she is indeed punishing Robbie.) Essential Feature 2, Developmentally and Culturally Appropriate Learning Environment, helps programs ensure that policies support the provision of an engaging curriculum that is meaningful to children.

Consider again Mrs. K's response to Robbie's behavior in our revised vignette when she empathizes with him about his rough morning, labels his emotions, and then suggests that he go look at the new train puzzle in the block area. In this case, Mrs. K. is enacting a humanistic approach to behavior guidance, as she is teaching Robbie to use words to name emotions and is supporting him to transition into the classroom after a rough morning. By ensuring that the curriculum and materials meet his developmental level and interests, she is also supporting his continued success in the block area.

When considering the function of children's behavior and what the behavior is communicating, it is important to remember that behavior can serve multiple purposes. Let's look again at what happens in the original vignette when Robbie walks over to the science center:

As Robbie walked to the science center, he pushed Jamar, who was building with Legos at the Lego table, causing Jamar's structure to fall over. After comforting Jamar and helping him pick up the Lego pieces, Mrs. K walked over to the science center. When Robbie saw Mrs. K approach, he ripped a poster of the four seasons off the wall and pushed the scale off the table. "That's it, Robbie, this behavior is not okay. We don't hit our friends and it is not okay to destroy property. You need to go to the quiet area and think about what you have done." Robbie glared at her, slowly walking to the quiet area, where he remained until his mother picked him up after receiving a call from the principal.

Robbie's behavior gets the teacher to pay attention to him (remember children's attention-seeking behaviors can be positive or negative) and serves another important function: escape. Robbie escapes going to the science table *and* gets to go sit by himself in the quiet area until his mother picks him up. After a frustrating morning and an unsympathetic, demeaning greeting from a coworker, wouldn't you rather escape to your office than dive right into the workday? Wouldn't you just rather go home? It is important to remember that most often children resort to challenging behavior because it *works*.

By using strategies described in the tiered models of support described in Essential Feature 4, teachers can learn to interpret behaviors using the ABC's (antecedents, behaviors, and consequences) of functional behavior analysis. When teachers approach children's behavior as communication of an unmet need rather than as an intentional act of defiance, the behavior becomes less personal, and it is easier to focus on teaching rather than reacting.

In the alternate scenario in which Mrs. K. reads Robbie's cues and helps him successfully transition to a new activity, she uses

A Humanistic Approach to Child Guidance

her relationship with him to understand and meet his needs. Because of her relationship with Robbie, Mrs. K. is able to uncover the meaning of his behavior before it escalates (prevention), while supporting him to self-regulate his behavior (teaching). In this way, Mrs. K. helps to open the door *with* Robbie by providing compassion and guidance.

Reframing our understanding of challenging behavior as communication is critical if we are to write and implement program policies that reflect the goal of an effective behavior-

guidance policy: to support all children's social, emotional, and academic success. Recalling the tiered models of support introduced in chapter one, the type of support and guidance children need to learn these social acceptable behaviors will vary based on each child's individual needs and circumstances. Children who have experienced early childhood trauma, for example, will most likely require an intensive, individualized approach. The need to view children as individuals is central to the fourth assumption of the TAG-PEC, that each child is a unique individual.

Each Child Is a Unique Individual

Now that we have reframed our understanding of challenging behavior to reflect the idea that challenging behavior is communication, it is important to consider each child as a unique individual. Think for a minute about your own children, your sibling(s), or two children that you know very well. How are these children the same? How are they different? From doing this exercise with our students over the years, and from our own experiences as parents, we know that many siblings are complete opposites of one another and that two children raised in the same household can be dramatically different in terms of temperament, energy level, motivation level, and interests. *Individual differences* is the term used to describe the multiple characteristics that distinguish us from one another and make us unique. The figure at right illustrates just a few of these characteristics.

When we think about challenging behaviors, it is critical that we take these individual differences into consideration. For example, whenever Sarah is asked to observe a child

Figure 3. Individual Differences

with challenging behaviors, the first thing she asks is, "How old is the child? What can you tell me about the child's language skills?" Age and language skills are just two examples of the many, many characteristics that make each child special.

It is also critical to note, as illustrated in Figure 4 below, that children develop in multiple contexts, including their family, their community, and public policy, and that these contexts interact in complex and dynamic ways.

Figure 4. The Child Develops in the Context of the Family, Community, and Public Policy

The case of Robbie is a perfect example of this. Robbie's vignette was modeled after an experience Sarah had while observing in a preschool classroom during her time as a Head Start administrator. While she had originally planned to stay in the classroom for only a short time, she ended up staying through lunch and until the children were asleep for nap to help the teachers with Robbie's challenging behavior, which continued to escalate as the morning progressed. (The child was not sent home as depicted in the vignette, as sending children home was a violation of program policy.) As she was leaving the center, feeling tired, hungry, and overwhelmed, a staff person shared that Robbie had been coming to school late for the past several days because the family car had broken down and Robbie's father had to bring him to school on the bus, after walking

the older siblings to school. Tiered models of support refer to this as a *setting event*. A setting event is something that occurs at another time and increases the likelihood that a child will engage in challenging behavior. In this way, setting events set the child up to have challenging behavior. In our example of arriving late to work, for example, all the events that transpired that morning set you up to (possibly) throw your coffee cup across the room. It is important to remember that a setting event can be observable or measurable (the child is sick, tired, or hungry), as in Robbie's case. Setting events can also be difficult to detect, as in the case of the residual effects of trauma, which we will discuss in chapter seven.

When Sarah returned to the center several days later, the same staff person shared that Robbie's father had let her know that his wife had recently relapsed and had been taking drugs again. These two pieces of information (broken-down car and the family situation) provided critical insight into the causes, or function, of Robbie's behavior. His normal schedule was off because of the broken-down car, and he was dealing with multiple stressors related to his mother's addiction. Importantly, and recalling our contention that children continue to engage in challenging behavior because it works, Robbie's behavior ensured that he would get what he wanted most, to be sent home where he could be with and get (most likely negative) attention from his mother. As this scenario hopefully illustrates, children with challenging behaviors need empathy, understanding, and support rather than punishment. Consider for a moment what the door to Robbie's future looks like in the first vignette in which Robbie gets sent home. What future do you envision for him? What future do you envision for Robbie in the second vignette?

Essential Feature 5, Working with Families, addresses ways in which families can be embedded in meaningful ways throughout behavior-guidance policies to ensure they are true partners in the process of dealing with challenging behaviors. Unfortunately, in our review of program policies, the need to involve families was addressed by the majority of programs only *after* the challenging behaviors had begun. We know from our experiences in the field that working with families, especially those whose children exhibit challenging behaviors, can be one of the most difficult aspects of working with young children. Effective, high-quality behavior-guidance policies can be an important tool for helping to ensure that parents become part their child's success in school. Our humanistic approach implores us to consider how we can also support families to be the best they can be. Essential Feature 5 of the TAGPEC helps guide programs to write and implement policies that include parents from the beginning (preventative) not just after things have gotten out of control (reactive).

In addition to the familial context, it is important to consider how economic, language, or immigration policies and contexts may be affecting the children in your program. While the discussion of the complex ways in which community and public policy impact children's development is beyond the scope of this book, it is critical to remember that children's behavior is the result of the dynamic interplay between multiple, complex contexts. Essential Feature 6, Staff Training and Professional Development, and Essential Feature 7, Use of Data for Continuous Improvement, help programs craft policies that support practices that are fair and equitable for all children while taking into consideration the individual characteristics and family community, and public policy contexts that make each child unique. These essential features also help programs create systems that support staff to understand the role of implicit bias on decision making, the final assumption of the TAGPEC.

Implicit Bias Affects Decision Making

Everyone has implicit biases about children and their behavior. *Implicit biases* are the unconscious beliefs and stereotypes that are made unintentionally and unknowingly (Banks, Eberhardt, and Ross, 2006). Recently, there has been a great deal of attention given to understanding how implicit bias affects the decisions we make, and researchers have identified a connection between high rates of preschool suspension and expulsion and the implicit bias of teachers (Gilliam, 2016). A humanistic approach to behavior guidance requires that we work to acknowledge and address implicit bias when dealing with challenging behaviors, and a goal of the TAGPEC is to help programs to enact policies that

support teaching staff and other school personnel to engage in this often difficult work.

Implicit bias influences our perceptions, interactions, behaviors, and feelings toward others in ways that we are unconscious of. For example, and recalling our earlier discussion of individual differences, Sarah remembers a discussion she had with one of her friends whose preschooler happened to be very tall for her age. Because the child's teachers unconsciously expected the child to be more mature both socially and academically, the mother intentionally put her child in ponytails with ribbons to remind the teachers that her child was only four years old.

Another example is that once a child exhibits challenging behavior, his teacher may expect him to act out regularly and may automatically interpret behaviors and cues as hostile. Implicit biases occur automatically and are the result of how we were raised, our daily experiences, and the media, all of which affect how we perceive information, make judgements about people and situations, and make decisions. Unfortunately, these unintentional biases can put the most vulnerable children at risk for being punished more often and more harshly. Boys, children with disabilities, and children of color, for instance, are all more likely to be perceived by teachers as misbehaving more frequently, even when the frequency of their misbehaviors is similar to that of their peers (Gilliam, 2016; Colker and Waterstone, 2011). Evidence also suggests that teachers' responses to children's behaviors that are based on implicit bias influence the disproportionality in disciplinary practices for children of color (McIntosh, Barnes, Eliason, and Morris, 2014; Milner, 2011; Monroe, 2009; Skiba et al., 2002; Togut, 2011). For example, a teacher may be quicker to judge that a student is "out of control" if that student is an African American boy.

Because implicit bias often affects the decisions we make, especially when we are faced with the stress and emotion that often accompany children's challenging behaviors, it is essential that early childhood educators intentionally and systematically work to identify and address implicit bias. Returning to the key assumptions of the TAGPEC can interrupt these decision points and remind us of our role to teach children social and emotional skills and more socially acceptable ways of getting their needs met. For example, viewing behavior as communication reframes children's behavior in ways that challenge our implicit biases. When we take the time to deconstruct what Robbie's behavior means and consider his uniqueness as an individual and the contexts in which he is embedded, we go from seeing him as an angry, out-of-control African American boy who is big for his age and maybe dangerous to a four-year old child who just wants to be with his mother. Being aware of and taking time to reflect on how children's behaviors trigger us, while keeping in mind our ultimate goal of teaching, can help us view children's behavior more equitably. Implicit bias and the alarming data on the discipline gap has led us to devote an entire chapter to the issue of language and culture and how the TAGPEC can be used to develop policies that support the implementation of practices that are fair, equitable, and culturally competent.

Reframing Our View of Challenging Behavior

Thus far, our goal has been to encourage you to reframe your understanding of discipline and to understand that the role of adults is to teach children the skills they need to be successful. A humanistic approach to behavior guidance is essential if we are to focus on teaching and guidance, which are at the core of the TAGPEC. In the following chapter, we will encourage you to think a bit deeper about this approach, as we consider how program guidance policies must value children's language and culture and see them as central to a systematic and intentional approach that is grounded in the belief that all children can be successful.

Culture and
Language

In diversity there is beauty and there is strength.

—Maya Angelou, author

"For the optimal development and learning of all children, educators must accept the legitimacy of children's home language, respect (hold in high regard) and value (esteem, appreciate) the home culture, and promote and encourage the active involvement and support of all families, including extended and nontraditional family units." This statement is from the National Association for the Education of Young Children's (NAEYC)'s position statement, "Responding to Linguistic and Cultural Diversity Recommendations for Effective Early Childhood Education," and reflects the importance of embracing cultural and linguistic diversity in early childhood programs. Viewing children's diversity as a strength is central to our humanistic approach to behavior guidance and is essential to the development and implementation of effective and equitable behavior-guidance policies.

Chang (2006) has proposed that culturally competent early childhood programs share the following eight characteristics:

- Skilled and effective teachers

- Low teacher-child ratios and appropriate group sizes

- Age-appropriate curriculum

- Engaged families

- Well-designed facilities

- Linkages to comprehensive services

- Culturally and linguistically appropriate assessment

- Available and accessible bilingual education services

While the purpose of this book is not to explore the complex interplay among language, culture, and early childhood settings, we believe that the five assumptions of our approach to behavior guidance and the seven essential features of the TAGPEC can help programs develop policies that build on the strengths that children bring with them into early childhood programs. Given the increasing diversity of children in early childhood programs and the troubling rates of suspension and expulsion based on race, which has been highlighted by research, it is imperative that we consider how language and culture can influence behavior—both children's and our own.

The purpose of this chapter is to describe how early childhood programs can use high-quality behavior-guidance policies to support culturally responsive practices and decision making that is equitable for all children. Let's begin by considering the following scenario:

It is Paola's second week attending a preschool program for four-year-olds at her local elementary school. She has no siblings, and prior to coming to school, her grandmother cared for her while her parents worked.

The teacher has noticed that Paola enjoys working in the writing center and is able to write most of the letters of her name. However, Paola has a difficult time transitioning from the writing center to clean-up time. Yesterday, when the teacher tried to show her how to clean up the materials, Paola pinched the teacher and crawled under the table, refusing to move and screeching in a high-pitched tone.

How can we use our humanistic approach to behavior guidance to help understand Paola's behavior? How can a high-quality behavior-guidance policy be used to create an infrastructure that supports children's social, emotional, and academic success? A great starting place is our belief that the role of early childhood educators is to teach.

The Role of the Adult Is to Teach Children Appropriate Social-Emotional Skills—But What's Appropriate?

Children acquire cultural knowledge beginning at birth and enter early childhood programs with understandings about how the world works based on interactions and experiences with family and community members. Perhaps the best example of this comes from the work of Shirley Brice Heath, a linguistic anthropologist who wrote the book *Ways with Words: Language, Life, and Work in Communities and Classrooms.* Heath studied the home-language practices of children and families living in several different communities located in close proximity to one another in the southeastern United States. She identified the various ways in which parents socialize their children to use language. Take a minute to read Heath's description of the language-socialization practices observed in two of the communities she studied:

> "Language and culture are the frameworks through which humans experience, communicate, and understand reality."
>
> —Lev Vygotsky, psychologist

Roadville

Residents of Roadville are primarily white, working-class families who have a long history of working in the local textile mill. Children are taught to work hard, respect authority, and attend church. Families believe that as long as they get their children to school each day, it is the teachers' responsibility to educate their children. Mothers in Roadville use baby talk with infants but correct their children's language as they get older because they believe that children need to "talk right" to be prepared for school. Play and the use of educational toys are valued as opportunities to promote language development. Memorization and repetition are important activities at home and at church, and children are expected to answer questions and perform for adults. Storytelling emphasizes correctness and attention to details and chronology, reflecting church-related practices. When children tell stories, they imitate the style used by adults, which focuses on telling true accounts of real events.

Trackton

Trackton is a predominantly African American working-class community whose residents have recently begun working in the mills after having traditionally made their living as farmers. Trackton is a small community that believes everyone should be involved in child rearing. Infants are rarely talked to directly by adults and are constantly physically held and comforted. Heath identified three stages that children between the ages of twelve and twenty-four months go through while learning how to have conversations with others: repetition, repetition with variation, and participation. Children are encouraged to look at contextual clues, such as body language, to develop responses to questions and statements. Boys learn how to use language by being challenged by older members of the community (usually men), while girls learn through "fussing" or singing play songs with older girls. Fictionalization in stories, or "talking junk," is encouraged, and good storytellers are valued members of the community. Children are talked to rather than read to and are encouraged to be creative storytellers. Flexibility and adaptability are the most important characteristics of learning.

Neither the children of Roadville nor of Trackton are successful in school, despite both communities placing a high value on school success and urging their children "to get ahead" by doing well in school. Health also studied the language-socialization practices of families living in another community, which she called Maintown, described below.

Maintown

Maintown has a suburban, mostly white, middle-class population and is where the schoolteachers and the managers of the mills live. Children in Maintown are treated as potential conversationalists beginning at birth, and mothers are their primary caregivers. Parents use baby talk and question-and-answer routines when talking with infants and young children. The residents of Maintown use reading and writing in ways that directly mirror the expectations of school, including how to use written sources to find information and how to use this information in their own writing. Members of the community participate in reading and writing for both work and leisure.

Now ask yourself the following questions:

1. Which children will enter a school setting in which language practices reflect what they have learned at home?

2. How might the children of Trackton respond if asked to retell a story told to them by an adult? How might the children of Roadville respond? Which of these responses best reflects the expectations of school?

3. How would the children of Roadville do on a creative-writing assignment? How would the children of Trackton do?

4. How do parents in Maintown socialize their own children to use language?

Heath's work highlights the variation in the language-socialization practices of different cultural communities and illustrates that, for many children, the disconnect between home and school begins at birth. Her work also illustrates how parents socialize their children to be successful members of their own community. In Trackton, for example, community residents value a good storyteller and teach their children how to play with words and be creative. The focus is not on the "correct" retelling of a story but on spontaneity and cleverness. Parents in Maintown and Roadville, on the other hand, value children being able to give the correct answer to a question posed by an adult, an ability expected and rewarded in school.

Socializing children into the culture of school, while at the same time respecting and valuing the home culture, is an important and difficult task. Early childhood educators must intentionally support children to become members of the classroom community and to learn the culture of school, even as they respect and honor the way things are done at home. It is critical to remember that children in early childhood classrooms are still learning the rules of school—how things work, what is expected of them, and how to act in ways that reflect the values and goals of the school setting. While there are undoubtedly individual differences among schools, the school system in the United States most often reflects the dominant European-American culture that values independence, individualism, and self-reliance. These traits reflect the goals of an individualist society and may be at odds with the goals and values of collectivist cultures, which tend to value interdependence and group success, adherence to norms and group consensus, and respect for authority and hierarchical roles (Trumbull, Rothstein-Fisch, and Greenfield, 2000).

With regard to the school setting, in *collectivist cultures* the role of the teacher is to transfer knowledge to students in a way that is clear, structured, and direct. The teacher has the knowledge, and it is her responsibility to transmit this knowledge to the children in the classroom. It is the children's responsibility to listen attentively and respect the teacher's authority. Because group harmony and interdependence are important goals of collectivist societies, children are expected to share and help one another with tasks.

Conversely, in an *individualist culture*, the focus is more on individual achievement than group success. The teacher expects students to be active participants and actively seek out knowledge through discussion and inquiry and to ask questions and have opinions that may contradict or challenge the views of the teacher. The following table provides examples of teaching practices associated with individualist and collectivist cultural perspectives.

Table 2: Individualist and Collectivist Cultural Perspectives on Education

Individualist Perspective	Collectivist Perspective
• Students work independently; helping others may be considered cheating.	• Students work with peers and provide assistance when needed.
• Students engage in discussion and argument to learn to think critically.	• Students are quiet and respectful in class so they can learn more efficiently.
• Property belongs to individuals, and others must ask to borrow it.	• Property is communal.
• The teacher manages the school environment indirectly and encourages student self-control.	• The teacher is the primary authority, but peers guide each other's behavior.
• Parents are integral to a child's academic progress and participate actively.	• Parents yield to the teacher's expertise to provide academic instruction and guidance.

Source: Adapted from LAB at Brown University. 2002. "Cultural Value Orientations: Collectivism and Individualism." *The Diversity Kit: An Introductory Resource for Social Change in Education.* Providence, RI: The Education Alliance, Brown University.

Culture and Language

It is important to remember that these perspectives on culture are very broad and that there is tremendous variation within cultural communities, as illustrated by the residents of Maintown and Roadville described by Heath. Although the families living in these communities were white and lived in the same region, they had different goals for their children, and the child-rearing practices used to achieve these goals were quite different. It is also important to consider the cultural practices of children from nondominant cultures, such as the African American families described by Heath. While there is tremendous diversity in African American families, some common characteristics have been identified by researchers. Because African American children are often raised in extended families, they are given many opportunities for social interaction (Hale, 1983; McLoyd et al., 2005) and are often sensitive to nonverbal communication, are good at interpreting facial expressions, and are emotionally expressive (Shade and Edwards, 1987). In addition, many African American families are deeply religious (Walsh, 2008), and their use of corporal punishment when disciplining children stems from feelings of love and concern, especially for African American boys (Boyd-Franklin, 2003).

When considering the cultural and socialization practices of families from nondominant cultures, it is critical to consider the roles of racism, prejudice, oppression, and segregation on the development of minority children and families (García Coll et al., 1996; Lindsey et al., 2007), and we have included information about this in the Resources section of the book.

When children from collectivist or nondominant cultures enter school for the first time, there is often a cultural mismatch between how children are socialized at home and how children are expected to behave at school. What happens when the culture of school does not match the culture of home?

Let's use this idea of a cultural mismatch to understand Paola's behavior. Is it possible that Paola is confused by the teacher's request to stop and clean up because Grandma lets her draw for hours at home and has always cleaned up for her? Sarah recalls her shock when, as a Head Start teacher, she observed a mother carrying her three-year-old son into the classroom. She was further surprised several days later when she made a home visit to see the child being spoon fed in a high chair. Not only were these child-rearing practices dramatically different from those Sarah was used to, they were also at odds with both the Head Start requirement that children serve themselves during meals and state early learning standards promoting the development of independence and self-help skills. While the parent who carried and spoon-fed her son was socializing him to be a successful member of a cultural community that values interdependence, educational settings in the United States and other Western cultures are designed to help students become successful in the dominant culture that values independence and autonomy. Following are several examples of how different cultural communities socialize children to become competent members of their culture and how these practices may be at odds with what is expected at school.

Table 3: Socialization Practices of Different Cultural Communities

European-American Culture	Collectivist Cultures
• Students are expected to work independently and to compete for rewards (Trumbull et al., 2001).	• Collectivist cultures, which may include children of recent immigrants, socialize their children to help one another learn (Delpit, 1995; Hale, 2001) and to "fit in, not stand out" (Trumbull et al., 2001).
• Talking with other students is discouraged (Shade, Kelly, and Oberg, 1997).	• In cultures that value interdependence, direct eye contact is considered rude (Trumbull et al., 2001).
• Students listen quietly while the teacher talks, and when they're called on, students respond one at a time by asking or answering questions. (Gay, 2000; Kochman, 1985).	• Children may be reluctant to speak in public as they are expected to watch and listen because adults are regarded as the source of knowledge (Trumbull et al., 2001).
• Students are expected to sit still and maintain eye contact to show that they are paying attention (Gay, 2000; Kochman, 1985).	• Some African American children learn through intense social interaction, which is a collaborative process. A speaker is often viewed as a performer who is making a statement, and while she's speaking, listeners join in and respond with gestures, movement, and words. The discourse is fluid, creative, and emotional, and no one needs permission to enter the conversation (Gay, 2000; Kochman, 1985). • Some African American families encourage children to assert themselves and display their energy, exuberance, and enthusiasm (Gay, 2000).
• European-American students are rewarded for answering "known answer" questions: questions that they and the adult already know the answer to, such as what color is your shirt and what is 4 + 6? Known-answer questions serve to highlight children's intelligence when they provide the correct answer.	• Some African American children may find known-answer questions confusing, as adults in their community often ask questions to challenge them or to learn new information. Children demonstrate their wit and intellect by responding spontaneously and creatively, not by providing a correct answer (Heath, 1983; Meier, 1998).
• Children raised in the dominant, middle-class culture are accustomed to implicit commands that tell students what to do indirectly, such as, "Miles, would you like to answer question number six?" Or, "Olivia, would you like to come to the front and show us the letter *O*?"	• Children from working-class homes, regardless of ethnicity, are often accustomed to direct, explicit commands, such as, "Ethan, show me the letter *E*." When faced with implicit commands, they may not realize the teacher isn't asking them a question or offering them a real choice and that there are consequences if they don't comply (Delpit, 1995).

Culture and Language

Within-Group Differences

When considering language and culture, it is also critical that we don't place children and families in boxes based on their linguistic and cultural heritage (Guitierrez and Rogoff, 2006). For example, while it is useful for a teacher to seek information on traditional child-rearing practices in China when he or she has a Chinese child in the classroom, it can be dangerous to assume that all Chinese families have the same goals for their children or socialize them in the same way. Families from rural China may socialize children differently than families coming from an urban setting, and factors such as religion and acculturation status may also affect how parents raise their children. *Acculturation* is the process and stress of cultural change that is experienced by members of a minority culture as they adapt to the majority culture of their new home. While Tables 3 and 4 identify several differences in expectations for children's behavior and ways of showing knowledge related to culture, we must be careful not to assume that just because families come from a similar linguistic or cultural background they share the same values or socialize their children in the same way. Culturally responsive teaching requires that we seek to understand not only within-child differences but also within-group differences that make each family unique. For example, although the Mexican-heritage families Sarah worked with in the inner city shared many traits and cultural practices with those she worked with in a nearby suburb, there were also many differences that were due primarily to immigration status and acculturation level. We have found the stages of acculturation, listed in Table 4 on page 37, to be particularly helpful when considering the acculturation status of young children and their families.

So what can teachers and administrators do to help teach children the norms and expectations of school while at the same time respecting and valuing the home culture? How can we support a child to be her best possible self as she is trying to make sense of multiple expectations for behavior while still learning important skills such as self-regulation and how to use increasingly complex language? Above all else, how can we help children develop a positive self-identity that incorporates both their home and school cultures?

Code Switching

The concept of code switching can be very useful in helping us understand how to support young children to successfully negotiate the overlapping worlds of home and school. With respect to language, code switching occurs when a speaker alternates between two or more languages, dialects, or registers in the context of a single conversation. Young dual-language learners, for example, might say, "Da me mi shoes" (Give me my shoes), and it is common practice for bilingual adults to alternate languages within a single conversation or sentence. Having just moved to southern California from the East Coast, Sarah remembers her surprise when, during her first staff meeting at Head Start, her colleagues switched from English to Spanish in the middle of a sentence. Code switching also refers to our ability to adjust the register of our speech depending on context—we have one way of speaking in professional contexts, another when out with our friends on a Friday night, and yet another when we speak to our grandmother or child. Code switching is normal and serves an important function as children learn a new language; it

Table 4: Stages of Acculturation

Stage	Feelings, Thoughts, Actions	Examples
Isolation	• Feeling disconnected • Feeling depressed • Experiencing culture shock • Having significant difficulty speaking the new language	Gabriela comes to Illinois from Guatemala with her four-year-old daughter. Her one-year-old has remained in Guatemala with her grandmother until Gabriela can afford to have them join her. Gabriela has few friends and is having difficulty finding a job because of language barriers.
Adaptation	• Increased comfort with immediate surroundings • Maintaining own traditions • Increased ability to teach others from one's own culture about mainstream culture	Gabriela attends a weekly prayer meeting at her local church. She frequently gives advice to other mothers about how to get along in the new country, including how to enroll their children in school and where to take ESL classes.
Biculturalism	• Feeling equally comfortable in one's own group and the mainstream culture • Maintaining important traditions from one cultural group and incorporating new traditions from mainstream culture	Gabriela works in a large corporate office where she is a successful sales manager. She practices many of her family's cultural traditions at home. She speaks English at work and Spanish at home and moves comfortably between two cultures.
Assimilation	• No longer practicing traditional cultural activities • Language of origin is not the language most spoken at home • Surroundings and social group reflect majority culture	Gabriela and her family celebrate Anglo cultural traditions and holidays. She maintains no connection with her home country, and she and her family are monolingual English speakers.

Source: Adapted from Casa de Esperanza. 2003. *Latino Families and Domestic Violence*. Minneapolis, MN: Casa de Esperanza.

helps humans seek to make meaning and connect with one another. Molinsky (2007) uses the term *cross-cultural code switching* to describe the task of moving between culturally ingrained systems of behavior. Our ability to code switch as adults allows us to negotiate the different contexts in which we may need to use a different "ways of being" to adapt to our current situation. Think for a moment about how you may navigate your own overlapping identities and how the ability to do so is an important part of who you are. For example, are you a confident, take-charge administrator during the week, but a more traditional wife and mother when you go to church on Sunday? Cultural code switching is an adaptive tool that allows individuals to handle or negotiate more than one identity and make connections with others. Importantly, the ability to code switch allows us, and children, to be citizens of an increasingly interconnected and diverse world. We have provided additional information about code switching in the Resources section of this book, and we encourage you to use it as part of your ongoing professional development efforts.

Let's consider for a moment how code switching is related to behavior and behavior guidance. Code switching is an observable behavior that sends a message about our internal state. Children are actually adept at doing this and learn from an early age which parent or other adult to seek out based on what they need or want. Is it possible for Paola to learn that with Grandma she doesn't have to clean up, but when she is at school she does? Absolutely! Think for a minute of your own children or children that you know very well—do they know to go to Mom for some things and Dad for others? Do they learn that Grandma will let them play all day while Uncle Tony means business? Children learn various ways to communicate their messages both at home and at school and to navigate the various contexts they encounter—they learn how to code switch.

Supporting children to feel good about and successfully negotiate their multiple identities is a critical task of the early childhood educator. Janet Gonzalez-Mena (2001) notes, "Only when professionals understand culturally sensitive care and are in close communication with families can they know how to work toward positive outcomes for children's identity, sense of belonging, and cultural competence."

Unfortunately, a great deal of research shows that when children from diverse backgrounds enter school, they receive powerful, negative messages about their home culture and language. While doing research for her dissertation, for example, Sarah studied a preschool in which two of the teachers were bilingual in both Spanish and English, and 98 percent of the children spoke Spanish at home. One of the teachers used both languages in her classroom and made sure there were many fun and engaging activities conducted in the children's home language as well as English. The second teacher, however, spoke Spanish to the children only when she needed to manage their behavior or give directions. While the children knew she spoke Spanish, they also knew she chose not to most of the time. Think for a moment about the messages each teacher's approach sent to the children about the value of their home language. Which teacher opened the door to a future in which the children could successfully navigate multiple identities, cultures, and languages and feel good about their biculturalism and bilingualism? While the teachers and children shared a common language in the center described above, there are many strategies available to help teachers value the home language and culture of young children if they do not share a common language. More information about this can be found in the Resources section of this book.

When teachers are culturally responsive, they connect children's cultural heritage to the early childhood setting, validate children's identities, and reinforce pride in their culture (Gay, 2010) while at the same time teaching them the expectations of school. We have included information about the Quality Benchmark for Cultural Competency Tool developed by NAEYC in the Resources section of this book, as it is an excellent resource for programs seeking to ensure that behavior-guidance policies and program practices reflect a strengths-based approach to language and culture.

When considering how to best teach children from diverse cultural and linguistic backgrounds, it is critical to remember that young children are in the process of developing their sense of self and lack the cognitive abilities to think logically and abstractly about issues such as race, culture, and language. What they do know, however, is how we as adults make them *feel,* and the messages that we send them about both their home and the dominant culture can have lifelong consequences on how they view the world and themselves. Consider for a moment the following quote from the Russian psychologist Lev Vygotsky: "It is through others that we develop into ourselves."

Children learn to value (or not value) who they are through their relationships with others, and the second assumption of our approach can be used to understand how teachers can use their relationships with children to help children feel proud of their home language and culture while at the same time teach them what is expected in the school setting.

Relationships Guide and Regulate Behavior

For early childhood teachers to build responsive and respectful relationships with children, they must both learn about the cultural and linguistic backgrounds of the children in their classrooms and understand how their own cultural background affects their view of children and families. As we mentioned in chapter two, the TAGPEC is grounded in the belief that child behavior is transactional and that both the teacher and child contribute to the relationship. As Sarah learned more about the families and children in her classroom, for example, it allowed her to reflect on how her own experiences growing up as part of the dominant culture influenced how she viewed (and judged!) the mother who carried and spoon fed her three-year old. As the year progressed, Sarah came to understand and respect how a mother carrying her son reflected the cultural value of *familismo,* which values the family as the primary source of one's identity and as protection against life's difficulties, as well as a belief in the importance of intergenerational ties and extended family systems. Importantly, Sarah also learned that there is more than one way to raise and socialize children.

What does this mean in an early childhood classroom? Consider for a moment a child who has difficulty transitioning to nap time in a preschool classroom. Nap time is often a difficult transition for both preschoolers and teachers, one that is made even more difficult because of children's individual biology—some children don't need to nap—and the fact that teachers take their lunch break while the children sleep. A child who doesn't go down for nap can easily be one of the most frustrating parts of the day for a teacher. Looking at this situation through a cultural lens, is it possible that the reason the child has difficulty getting on his cot is because he cosleeps with his parents or siblings at home? Perhaps his mother is scared to share this information with the teacher because she is embarrassed that they share an apartment with another family. Or perhaps she is afraid of being judged for her parenting practices that worked just fine in the family's home country?

> "Could a greater miracle take place than for us to look through each other's eyes for an instant?"
>
> —Henry David Thoreau, author

It takes time to get to know about children's families and culture, but doing so will only serve to strengthen relationships, which are essential if children are going to feel safe and ready to learn. The key here is that teachers and administrators actively reflect on their own cultural beliefs while seeking information about children and families—especially those that come from a different cultural and linguistic background than their own. Gonzalez-Mena (2008) highlights the need to question our assumptions about child-development practices by reminding ourselves that "My way of thinking about X is not the only way to think about it. My way of doing Practice Y is not the only way to work with the child." It is important to remember that while our role is to teach, it is also to learn.

Culturally Responsive Teaching and Guidance

Once teachers learn about children's cultural and linguistic heritage, they are better able to engage in culturally responsive teaching and guidance practices. Cultural responsiveness refers to the multidimensional and empowering recognition that children's cultural backgrounds are foundational to instruction, selection of materials, and interactions with children and families (Gay, 2010). What does this mean? When teachers learn about the individual strengths, interests, and skills of the children enrolled in their program, they can use this knowledge to plan and implement curriculum that builds on and reflects these strengths.

What might this look like for Paola's teacher? What strengths can the teacher leverage to help Paola be her best self? Let's take another look, paying particular attention to Paola's strengths.

It is Paola's second week attending a preschool program for four-year-olds at her local elementary school. She has no siblings, and prior to coming to school, her grandmother cared for her while her parents worked.

The teacher has noticed that Paola enjoys working in the writing center and is able to write most of the letters of her name. However, Paola has a very difficult time transitioning from the writing center to clean-up time. Yesterday, when the teacher tried to show her how to clean up the materials, Paola pinched the teacher and crawled under the table, refusing to move and screeching in a high-pitched tone.

Paola's interest in writing is an asset that the teacher can use to build a relationship with Paola while teaching her about the expectations of the classroom. For example, she might let Paola know that she needs some help and has a very important job for Paola to do because she is so good at writing her letters. Or, she may meet with Paola and her grandmother at pick-up time and explain that, because Paola is such a great writer, the teacher needs some special help with something very important in the classroom.

In this way, rather than greeting Grandma with news about Paola's bad behavior, she is using something that Paola does well to form a connection with the family.

The teacher might then sit with Paola at the writing center and help her make a sign that says *Clean-up time.* Five minutes before clean-up time (Here, she may bring Paola over to the visual schedule that has pictures of children cleaning up to give her a concrete example to go along with what she is saying.)

she will ask Paola to put away the writing things because she needs her to hold up her *Clean-up time* sign and walk around the classroom letting the other children know that it is time to clean up. To show respect for and continue to develop Paola's home language—while supporting the development of English—one side of the sign could say *Clean up time,* while the other could say *Tiempo de limpiar.* In this way, the teacher is valuing the home language and letting Paola know that Spanish plays an important role in helping the classroom community function smoothly.

It is important that we acknowledge that scenarios such as this are difficult, particularly in the absence of a shared language. Fortunately, there are many excellent resources that provide strategies programs can use to communicate and engage with families from diverse backgrounds, and we have provided several of them in the Resources section of this book.

Gay (2000) has described culturally responsive teaching as teaching to and through the strengths of children. In using Paola's strength to help her become part of the classroom routine by helping ensure that transitions are smooth, Paola's teacher is teaching rather than punishing and is being proactive rather than reactive, both of which are central to our humanistic approach. Next, let's look at what Paola's behavior could be communicating, using what we know about culturally responsive teaching.

Behavior Is Communication

We've already identified one possible reason for Paola's behavior—that she is confused by the request to stop and clean up because Grandma lets her draw for hours and has never expected her to clean up after herself. What other reasons could there be for Paola's behavior? Could it simply be that Paola is so engaged at the writing center that she doesn't want to clean up for lunch? Might this be typical, developmentally appropriate behavior for a four-, five-, or six-year-old? School in the United States is very fast paced and structured, which may lead to expectations for children's behavior that are not a great fit with individual characteristics such as temperament or community-held expectations about time. Perhaps Paola is overwhelmed by not understanding all of the English words being spoken in the classroom and is angry that the teacher does not pronounce her name the same way her family does. Taking the time to learn how to pronounce a child's name sends the message that the child's language, culture, and family are important and reaffirms a child's positive self-identity. Conversely, mispronouncing a child's name can negatively impact a child's self-image and cause the child to reject her home culture.

> "Every day, in a hundred small ways, our children ask, 'Do you hear me? Do you see me? Do I matter?' Their behavior often reflects our response."
>
> —L. R. Knost, author

Could Paola's behavior be the result of all of these things?

As we discussed in chapter one, young children are just learning how to express their complex feelings with words and to self-regulate their behavior. When faced with an unfamiliar language and conflicting cultural expectations, children may act out or shut down in an attempt to escape. When considering the meaning behind children's challenging behavior, it is essential to consider the role that a child's cultural and linguistic background may play. While embarrassing to admit, Sarah remembers volunteering in her son's kindergarten classroom and observing a child rocking back and forth with his head between his knees as the teacher conducted a circle-time writing lesson. At the time, Sarah thought, "Oh, that child must be autistic." As Sarah spent more time in the kindergarten classroom, she learned that the child only spoke Spanish and this was his first time in a school setting. Sarah's immediate judgement of this child is a perfect example of implicit bias and why it is essential that teachers and administrators reflect on how their bias can influence both attitudes and practices.

Returning to our assumption that relationships guide and regulate behavior, the early childhood teacher can serve as a bridge for a child's inner experience and her outward behavior. When teachers are in tune with children and can read their emotional cues, they can take steps to prevent challenging behavior before it occurs. Tiered models of support such as the Teaching Pyramid provide multiple strategies for helping children to self-regulate and express their emotions before they escalate. These strategies include the use of picture schedules, scripted stories, and classroom/ program-wide rules posted in visual form. Sometimes the child just needs to know that the teacher is nearby and is there for support if needed. Let's consider an alternate scenario for the child rocking back and forth in the kindergarten classroom.

Before transitioning the children from centers to the carpet for a whole-group writing activity, Mrs. H. leads Luis to the picture schedule posted on the wall. She explains that the class will be cleaning up and points to a picture showing all of the children cleaning up at the various centers. She then points to a picture of the children sitting down in the circle area and explains that the children will come to the carpet when they have finished cleaning up.

When the children come to circle, Mrs. H. makes sure that Luis is sitting up in the front near her. Because she knows that Luis and several other students enjoy going to the school garden, her writing lesson is about the garden and the green beans they saw growing during their last visit. Because of Luis's proximity to Mrs. H., she is able to keep him engaged in the activity by gently touching his leg or asking him to hold her marker for her. She has also intentionally planned her daily schedule so the children play outside following whole-group activities.

Many of the strategies described above are not only helpful for a dual-language learner like Luis but are also good child-development practice. Mrs. H. knows her students and considers their individual needs and interests as she plans her curriculum. Remembering that each child is unique is another assumption of our approach that helps educators to be culturally responsive.

Each Child Is a Unique Individual

Viewing each child as an individual is critical to our humanistic approach to behavior guidance. Over the years, we have had teachers and administrators tell us that making special accommodations for children, such as allowing Paola to take on a special role in the classroom or letting Luis sit up front and hold the teacher's marker, are not fair and reward children for their bad behavior. Perhaps the most distressing story we heard was from a preschool teacher, Rose, who was enrolled in a course we taught on the Teaching Pyramid.

Rose had worked very hard with a little girl in her classroom who had joined the class late in the year and had exhibited challenging behaviors. Rose had successfully used scripted stories to help this child regulate her behavior and learn what was expected of her during circle time and other parts of the day. (See the Center on the Social and Emotional Foundations for Early Learning (CSEFEL) website listed in the Resources section for more information about scripted stories.) When it came time to transition the child to kindergarten, Rose shared the scripted story with the child's new teacher, who responded by stating, "There is no way that I am going to reward the child by giving her a special book." Rose then told our class that the following year she often saw this child standing outside of the kindergarten classroom in time-out. Returning to our humanistic approach, we must ask ourselves whether denying extra support and placing a child in time-out helps her to be her best self.

> "Fairness does not mean everyone gets the same. Fairness means everyone gets what they need."
>
> —Rick Riordan, author

Fair Does Not Mean Equal

Truly valuing children (and adults!) as individuals means that we must realize that fair does not always mean equal. Ensuring that things are fair really means ensuring that each child knows that she is safe and has what she needs to be successful. We must also understand that these needs will vary from child to child and that when these needs are unmet, they often result in challenging behavior. Because this chapter is about language and culture, our next request may sound strange: Forget for a minute about culture and language and consider other within-person characteristics that make a child unique. We discussed some of these characteristics in chapter two, including learning style, gender, and temperament. Could Paola have a slow-to-warm temperament, making transitions even more difficult for her? Perhaps she is a visual learner, making it more difficult for her to follow the teacher's verbal request to clean up? When considering what makes children unique, it is critical that we consider every facet of the child's personality and not just focus on her culture or language. When we know that Paola is a dual-language learner, an only child, has a slow-to-warm temperament, is a visual learner, and comes from a culture that values interdependence, we get much more insight into what makes her tick. This insight opens the door for us to build a responsive and respectful relationship with her, understand possible reasons for her behavior, and develop and implement strategies that will teach her the social and emotional skills she needs to be successful. In addition to within-person characteristics, there are also factors outside of the child that make her unique, including her birth order, family socioeconomic status, immigration history, and the family's access to medical care. When taking all of these factors into consideration, it makes sense that the needs of each child will vary.

Avoiding a Tourist Approach to Diversity

Honoring children as individuals also requires that we avoid a tourist approach to valuing diversity. Louise Derman-Sparks (1993) uses the term *tourist multiculturalism* to describe curricular approaches that merely visit a culture rather than integrate children's cultures and experiences into the curriculum in meaningful and authentic ways throughout the year. A tourist approach to multicultural education is often driven by months or seasons of the year, such as "studying" Native Americans in November (the month of Thanksgiving in the United States) by having the children make headbands, or reading books about African Americans only during February (Black History Month in the United States). This approach trivializes, patronizes, and stereotypes cultures by focusing on traditional costumes, foods, and dances and by avoiding authentic pictures of the everyday life of the people from that culture (Derman-Sparks, 1993). Students exposed to a tourist approach to curriculum often come away from this experience with even more biases.

Placing chopsticks in the dramatic play area all year long is a much more responsive and respectful way to include the culture of a Chinese child in the classroom than celebrating Chinese New Year for one day in January. Similarly, displaying real photos of children and families is a much more respectful way to honor diversity than hanging a poster that shows cartoon children in a variety of costumes.

Take a close look at the faces of the children in the cartoon image. What do you notice? Do you know any real children who look like this in real life?

Children feel respected when they see themselves in the materials and activities provided in the classroom and when these activities are planned by thoughtful, intentional teachers who continually strive to help children feel safe, valued, and visible in the daily life of the classroom. Supporting teachers to do this is critical to the final assumption of our approach, bringing to the foreground the effect of implicit bias on decision making.

Implicit Bias Affects Our Decision Making

At the time Sarah made the judgement that the boy in her son's classroom was autistic, she was enrolled in an educational leadership doctoral program focused on social justice. This fact highlights the power of implicit bias—everyone has it. The world is a confusing place, and looking for patterns and seeking explanations for phenomena through our observations is an important part of how we learn and make sense, beginning at birth. Implicit bias is part of our automatic social cognition and arises even when a person has made an explicit commitment to social justice and egalitarianism. If educators do not actively seek to acknowledge and address these biases, the results for children can be enormous. Many studies offer evidence that suggests disciplinary practices are influenced by implicit bias (McIntosh, Barnes, Eliason, and Morris, 2014; Milner, 2011; Monroe, 2009; Skiba, et al., 2002; Togut, 2011).

Recently, Dr. Walter Gilliam from the Yale Child Study Center sought to find a possible explanation for the troubling rates of pre-school expulsion based on race and gender. In this study, preschool teachers were asked to watch video clips of students (who were actually actors who didn't misbehave) and to point out signs of "challenging behavior." Using eye-tracking technology, research-ers found that teachers spent more time looking at black children—especially black boys—than white children. Black teachers were found to hold black students to a higher standard of behavior than white teachers did. White teachers tended to be more lenient toward the behavior of children with stereo-typically black names such as LaToya or DeShawn. Gilliam suggests that this leniency is due to the fact that white teachers expect black students to misbehave.

Allen and Sneed (2016) recommend that, to effectively decrease implicit bias, teachers should participate in learning opportunities, including trainings, workshops, and coaching, and in reflection activities that make them aware of implicit bias; help them explore how the assumption of a Western, white, mid-dle-class worldview may affect their teaching practices; capitalize on their good intentions; and expose them to positive realities that counter negative stereotypes (Weinstein, Tomlinson-Clarke, and Curran, 2004).

To ensure that teachers have these types of opportunities, behavior-guidance policies must address staff training and professional development as well as the use of a data-collection system that helps to recognize,

acknowledge, and interrupt bias. We have included a pol-icy report based on Gilliam's study in the Resources section of this book, as well as a link to the Implicit Association Test (IAT), which was developed by researchers inter-ested in educating the public about hidden biases. Asking staff to take the IAT can be a great starting point for conversations about how implicit bias affects decision making when it comes to challenging behavior. In addition, Appendix B provides strategies to reduce implicit bias in the early childhood setting that have been developed by the Kirwan Institute at Ohio State University. We have aligned each of these strategies with the essential features of the TAGPEC to guide early childhood program leaders and their staff to think critically about how policy can help address implicit bias.

> "Expulsion is not a child behavior. It's an adult decision."
>
> —Walter Gilliam, child-development researcher

Research indicates that school policies, preservice training, and professional devel-opment often do not take into account the social and emotional needs of children from diverse backgrounds (Rashid, 2009; Vincent et al., 2011). The seven essential features of the TAGPEC and our humanistic approach can guide programs to develop policies that promote cultural and linguistic diversity as strengths and can encourage discourse about culture and language in the early child-hood setting. The tool also helps to ensure that culturally relevant practices are embed-ded into the curriculum and that systems are in place to examine data to ensure equitable practices that help all children to be their very best selves. In the following chapter, we pres-ent the research basis for the seven essential features and provide examples of how they can be written into policy.

The Research behind the Seven Essential Features of the TAGPEC

This chapter will be especially helpful to administrators who are interested in gaining a deeper understanding of the evidence supporting the high-quality guidance practices that we recommend incorporating into policy.

For each essential feature, we provide a brief synthesis of the research findings, followed by sample statements taken from real policies that illustrate the essential feature.

The Seven Essential Features of High-Quality Behavior-Guidance Policies

Behavior-guidance policies should:

1   reflect an instructional, proactive approach to guidance that supports the learning and practice of appropriate prosocial behavior.

2   describe the importance of a developmentally and culturally appropriate learning environment that is predictable, engaging, and relationship based.

3   describe clear and consistent expectations for behavior.

4   identify primary, secondary, and tertiary preventative and intervention practices for promoting prosocial behavior and reducing challenging behavior in young children.

5   reflect the family-centered nature of early childhood education.

6   ensure that staff have access to training and technical assistance in implementing policy guidelines and promoting the social competence of young children.

7   reference the use of a data-collection system by which the relative success or failure of the guidance policy will be evaluated.

Essential Feature 1: Intentional Focus on Teaching Social-Emotional Skills

Early childhood behavior-guidance policies should reflect an instructional, proactive approach to behavior guidance that supports the learning and practice of appropriate prosocial behavior of all children, regardless of individual differences and/or cultural and linguistic background.

In response to emerging research on discipline (e.g., Schweinhart et al., 2005; Zinns, Bloodworth, Weissberg, and Walberg, 2004) and legislation in schools (e.g., NCLB, 2001; IDEA, 2004), early childhood programs have been gradually moving toward a new paradigm for addressing challenging behaviors with young children. More specifically, there has been a shift from an emphasis on punitive, reactive approaches that focus mainly on managing children's behavior to more positive, proactive approaches that support the learning and practice of prosocial behavior. A major reason for this paradigm shift is the emerging research showing that punitive forms of discipline, when used in isolation, are ineffective in changing children's behavior over time (e.g., Garnes and Menlove, 2003; Sugai and Horner, 2002). In contrast, research on more positive forms of discipline suggests that these approaches are more effective in teaching children self-discipline in both the short and long run (Padden, 2009). This research reflects the first assumption of our approach, that if we want children to behave appropriately, then we need to teach them the appropriate behaviors.

Behavior-guidance policies need to emphasize the importance of teaching social norms and desired behaviors, positively acknowledging prosocial behavior in ways valued by children, and providing children with multiple and continued opportunities to use and practice those behaviors.

Early childhood professionals can both indirectly and directly support the learning and practice of positive behavior. Indirect guidance strategies include those related to environments, curriculum, and classroom rules. Direct guidance strategies include prompting children in naturalistic contexts and using natural and logical consequences, such as, "Pablo, I see you have finished your drawing. We will be ready to go outside when you put the crayons away"; modeling; redirection; rehearsing and role-playing; giving children choices, such as, "Sierra, I can't let you tear the pages in books. This is the second page you have torn today. You will need to make another choice instead of the reading corner. You may go to the block area or the art area. Which do you choose?" and acknowledging and reinforcing positive behavior when it does occur. Additional ways in which prosocial behavior can be taught are listed in Table 5.

Table 5: Strategies to Help Teach Prosocial Behavior

Strategy	Example
Positive commenting	"Joshua, you are such a kind friend. It made me feel so happy today when I saw you share the bucket with Micah when you were playing in the sandbox."
Asking children to brainstorm ways in which they can be responsible members of the classroom community	"Let's make a list of all of the things that we can do to make sure we take care of our classroom."
Helping children work through difficult situations	"Roberto and Jackson, I know that everyone wants to play with the new train tracks in the block area. Let's practice how to ask for a turn."

Behavior-guidance policies are an ideal place for a program to state its commitment to teaching children through positive forms of discipline. A policy that includes a statement about its positive, preventative approach to discipline conveys that the program is intentional in its approach to teaching appropriate social norms and desired behaviors. It also communicates to staff and families that behavior guidance is a priority within the program. Policy phrases that reflect an intentional approach to teaching often include language such as, "We *assist* children in learning to guide their own behavior," "We *help children learn* self-discipline," and "We *teach* children appropriate ways of behaving in the classroom."

Following is an excerpt from a behavior-guidance policy that clearly shows the program's commitment to an instructional, intentional approach. Often, statements about teaching approaches, such as the mission statement or philosophy, are found in a program's hand-book and can easily be adapted for inclusion in the behavior-guidance policy.

Sample Policy Statement Reflecting Essential Feature 1

One of the goals of the Children's Center program is to assist children in learning to guide their own behavior. The role of the teacher is to help children learn to eventually solve their own problems and to provide children with the tools to do so. Additional strategies that are used to promote children's learning of positive behavior include:

- Building relationships with children, families, and colleagues

- Designing engaging environments

- Establishing consistent and developmentally appropriate rules and routines

- Implementing developmentally and culturally appropriate learning activities and providing feedback and encouragement

- Modifying and adapting materials and activities to meet the individual needs of children

Essential Feature 2: Developmentally and Culturally Appropriate Learning Environment

Early childhood behavior-guidance policies should describe the importance of a developmentally and culturally appropriate learning environment that is predictable, engaging, and relationship based.

The classroom learning environment, which includes the physical layout, the curriculum, the schedule, and the teacher-child relationship, plays a critical role in promoting positive behavior by setting the stage for student engagement (Conroy, Davis, Fox, and Brown, 2002; Dunlap et al., 2003). Research shows that when children are actively engaged, teachers spend more time teaching and less time reacting to problem behaviors (Lynch and Simpson, 2010).

There are a number of guidance strategies that teachers can use to create a positive, developmentally and culturally appropriate classroom environment. For example, teachers can consider positive, developmentally and culturally appropriate strategies when they are arranging indoor or outdoor environments, such as ensuring materials reflect different ability levels, interests, and cultural backgrounds; routinely modifying indoor or outdoor environments, such as adding props to encourage social interaction; arranging temporal environments, such as allowing sufficient time for children to play and work at their own pace; and having classroom rules that are linked to behavioral expectations outlined in guidance policies. For example, the classroom rule "We listen to our friends and teacher" is linked to the policy behavioral expectation "We want children to positively participate in group activities." And perhaps the most important indirect strategy for reducing challenging behavior in young children is to implement a curriculum that engages all children in activities that hold their interests and stimulate their learning. When children are actively engaged, early childhood professionals will find that they spend more time teaching and less time reacting to problem behaviors.

Young children thrive when provided with a predictable schedule and consistent routines. When coupled with an organized environment and a hands-on, engaging curriculum that reflects the children's interests, the stage is set for children to be successful. An example of this comes from Sarah's experience as a literacy coach. A teacher approached her about behavioral concerns in the classroom, and during her initial observation, Sarah noticed that all of the furniture was pushed up against the walls, leaving a big open space in the center of the room. Indeed, several children were running and wrestling in this large open space. She then looked at the classroom schedule and saw that several of the children arrived at the center at five o'clock in the morning. (This was a center for children of low-income parents who were working or in school.) In addition, a forty-minute circle time followed breakfast, and Sarah observed that many of the children were fidgety and disruptive during this teacher-led activity.

Over the course of the next few weeks, Sarah and the teacher rearranged the classroom environment to create learning centers and clear pathways. The new arrangement signaled how children were to use the space and curbed their ability to run and wrestle. The classroom schedule was also changed to allow the children to go outside following breakfast. When the children returned inside at ten o'clock, they were ready to participate in a shorter, more child-centered and collaborative circle time.

An example of an excerpt from a behavior-guidance policy that reflects Essential Feature 2 is provided below. As with Essential Feature 1, this essential feature is often folded within the guidance policy's mission or philosophy section.

Sample Policy Statement Reflecting Essential Feature 2

Our staff use a positive guidance approach, which enables a child to develop self-control and assume responsibility for his or her own behavior. We stress the importance of establishing and fostering positive relationships among staff and children. We foster and guide a child's choices so his or her behavior will reflect peaceful human relationships with other children and adults. We provide an age-appropriate environment and curriculum that is stimulating. We carefully consider how to use children's cultural and linguistic backgrounds to engage the children in meaningful activities conducive to the development of a positive self-image in each child. We believe in following a simple yet consistent set of developmentally appropriate rules so that children can thrive in a predictable and secure environment.

Essential Feature 3: Setting Behavioral Expectations

Early childhood behavior-guidance policies should describe clear and consistent expectations for behavior.

Setting clear behavioral expectations at the program and classroom levels has been found to be critical to preventing and addressing challenging behaviors (Grisham-Brown, Hemmeter, and Pretti-Frontczak, 2005; Sugai and Horner, 2002). An important component of a high-quality guidance policy is a description of program-wide behavioral

expectations for young children that provides early childhood professionals and families with information about the desired behaviors (Council for Children with Behavior Disorders, 2002; Lewis and Sugai, 1999; Moldenhauer-Salazar, 2000; Strain and Joseph, 2004). Clearly written behavioral expectations help to ensure that "everybody's on the same page" and create a unified vision for socially valued behaviors. Guidance policies should describe behavioral expectations that are short and stated positively, letting the children know what they should do rather than what they should not do. Examples of behavioral expectations commonly used in early childhood classrooms include, "Be safe," "Be kind," and "Be responsible." These behavioral expectations can easily be translated into classroom rules that are both appropriate and meaningful for children of all ages. For example, a toddler teacher might tell a toddler who throws away her plate after lunchtime, "Lucinda, I like how you are throwing your plate away. You are so responsible!" A teacher of preschoolers may facilitate a circle-time discussion about what it means to be responsible for the classroom garden. Conversely, if a toddler hits another child and grabs her toy, the teacher can say, "Veronica, hitting Serena is not kind. We need to be kind to our friends and use our words when we want to play." When teachers use language to help children identify what they are feeling, the children are more likely to internalize and use emotion language themselves. Teachers can also help children learn words and phrases that will help them to solve their problems during direct instruction, such as during book reading, role-playing, or games.

Expectations for behavior also need to be appropriate, reflecting the natural learning abilities typically associated with the age groups of the children. For example, while most toddlers engage in hitting, kicking, pushing, and shoving for short periods of time, these are age-appropriate behaviors for children who are still learning the rules of social interaction. When behavioral expectations are stated positively—"Be safe"—teachers can describe to children what this looks like across settings and can support the development of self-regulation and other social-emotional skills. An example of an excerpt from a guidance policy that reflects Essential Feature 3 is provided below. Note that the statement is simple and concise yet conveys the program's approach to setting clear and developmentally appropriate behavior expectations. The expectations are also broad enough to be used program wide.

Sample Policy Statement Reflecting Essential Feature 3

Each class uses the same basic rules, which are as follows:

1   We keep ourselves safe. (We listen to the teacher; we stay with the group.)

2   We keep each other safe. (We use safe touches; we listen to one another.)

3   We keep our things safe.

Essential Feature 4: Preventing and Addressing Challenging Behaviors Using a Tiered Model of Intervention

Early childhood behavior-guidance policies should identify primary, secondary, and tertiary preventative and intervention practices for promoting prosocial behavior and reducing challenging behavior in young children.

Research suggests that adopting a continuum of prevention and intervention practices in early childhood programs results in positive outcomes for young children, their families, and the professionals who work with them (Dunlap, Fox, and Hemmeter, 2004; Forness et al., 2000). Primary practices focus on the use of specific adult-child interactions and environmental arrangements to teach and support prosocial behavior in *all* children. Examples of primary strategies include the provision of engaging and meaningful environments and curricula and responsive, respectful interactions between teachers and children. For example, if a preschool teacher notices that several of the children in her classroom have been interested in digging holes during outside play, she might intentionally include this interest in her curriculum planning. During circle time she would tell the children, "I am so happy to see all of you today! I have a big surprise. I know how much you are enjoying digging, and I have some special tools—called *trowels* and *spades*—to help you dig even deeper!"

Secondary practices include explicit and systematic instruction, such as the use of a social-skills curriculum or targeted individual and/or group interventions. Secondary strategies are helpful for all children but are particularly useful for small groups or individual children who need a little more support managing their behavior or expressing their emotions. For example, if a teacher observes that several children are having difficulty working together in the block area, he would gather the group together and have them role play what it looks like to be kind to friends when playing in this area. Or, he might develop a scripted story with pictures of a child transitioning from one activity to another, when an individual child has difficulties transitioning throughout the day.

At the tertiary level, early childhood professionals and families work collaboratively to define the challenging behavior of individual children, collecting contextually relevant information, such as what happens immediately

before and after the challenging behavior occurs and information about family routines, and jointly develop a plan to teach desired behaviors and decrease the problem behavior (Dunlap, Fox, and Hemmeter, 2004; Forness et al., 2000; Sugai and Horner, 2002).

When working as a literacy coach in the classroom described on page 51, for example, Sarah noticed that the preventative, primary strategies related to environment, routine, and curriculum were sufficient for many of the children, who quickly became engaged with classroom materials and internalized expectations and routines. For a small group of children, however, the use of secondary strategies was necessary to prevent and address challenging behavior. In this instance, Sarah worked with the teacher to collect documentation on when the challenging behavior occurred (time of day, setting, and frequency) and examined screening and assessment results to develop second-tier strategies that intentionally targeted identified challenges. Finally, when data indicated that primary and secondary strategies were not sufficient, a behavior plan was developed for two of the children to provide more intense, individualized support.

Often, programs will mention specific curricula, such as Second Step or Conscious Discipline, in their policy statements to further demonstrate their commitment to providing intentional social-emotional instruction. Mentioning a specific curriculum isn't necessary; what matters is that the program articulates a commitment to teaching social and emotional skills to all students, including those at risk for social and emotional problems. An example of an excerpt from a guidance policy that reflects Essential Feature 4 is provided below.

Sample Policy Statement Reflecting Essential Feature 4

The Children's Program will use three curriculum models in our classrooms as a way

to introduce and teach positive social skills. These curricula are *Pretend Public Schools*

Preschool Child Outcomes, Second Step, and *Talking about Touching.* Each of these curricula emphasizes safety and the importance of understanding how someone else feels. They teach children to recognize feelings of others and themselves, solve their own problems, and express their anger in nonviolent ways. Each curriculum emphasizes having the children practice and role play problem situations as they use them in everyday interactions.

Essential Feature 5: Working with Families

Early childhood behavior-guidance policies should reflect the family-centered nature of early childhood education.

Because the social and academic success of young children depends heavily upon active family involvement and the successful intervention of challenging behavior requires comprehensive interventions across home and school or program settings (Forgatch and Patterson, 1998; Grisham-Brown, Hemmeter, and Pretti-Frontczak, 2005; McEvoy and Welker, 2000; Sheldon and Epstein, 2002; Turnbull, Turnbull, Erwin, and Soodak, 2006; Webster-Stratton, Reid, and Hammond, 2001), behavior-guidance policies must reflect the family-centered nature of early childhood education. Programs that implement strong family-involvement programs have fewer discipline problems. If a behavior-guidance policy sees parents *only* as recipients of information, as in for example, "Parents will be contacted when an undesirable behavior pattern develops, and suspension may be necessary," it can impede the development of positive, proactive, and authentic collaborative relationships with families. Making sure that parents are aware of behavioral expectations *before* problems arise can be done by communicating behavioral expectations in the parent handbook and reviewing them during orientations. Many programs also post behavioral expectations as a visual reminder for staff, parents, and children.

Another way to adopt a preventative and collaborative approach with parents is to learn more about each child's home environment and how behavior is handled at home. For example, Margaret, a preschool teacher we worked with, described how three-year-old Alondra was having difficulty in the dramatic play area. The problems centered primarily on a sparkly, purple purse that Alondra did not want any other child to touch—even when she was playing in another area. After observing Alondra's behavior for a week, Margaret approached her mother and shared that while Alondra enjoyed playing in the dramatic play area with the other children, she got very upset when another child tried to play with the purse. Alondra's mother shared that prior to coming to the center, Alondra, who was an only child, had been cared for by her grandmother and was not used to being around other children. She also said that she had been struggling with Alondra's "feisty" personality at home. By working together, the teacher and parent were able to promote consistency across environments.

An example of an excerpt from a guidance policy that reflects Essential Feature 5 is provided below. This essential feature often merits its own section in a policy because there are multiple components including the program's approach to families, the program's communication style with families, and the program's plan for addressing challenging behaviors with families.

Sample Policy Statement Reflecting Essential Feature 5

The mission of the Children's Center is to provide developmentally appropriate, curriculum-based child care programs in a nurturing, loving, safe, and stimulating environment.

We believe that parents are the primary educators of the child. The home is the child's first and continual learning environment. Children come to school with different life experiences and skills that we acknowledge and draw upon as we plan for and facilitate new learning. Parents have an in-depth knowledge of their children. When parents share this knowledge, teachers can better understand each child.

We believe that parents are our partners. We recognize that a child's home is the first and most important place of learning. Any information you give us concerning your family culture, rituals, or challenges helps us better understand your child's needs. By becoming involved with the classroom, you are supporting our philosophy of partnership and are making a link between home and school. We invite your involvement in the classroom by helping out with a special activity, an ongoing activity, and/or on field trips.

We believe that communication is key. Communication on all levels is important. Families receive program and classroom-specific newsletters at least quarterly. Upcoming events and activities are posted

by the front door and on each classroom's bulletin board. Teachers make an effort to talk with each child's parent at least once a day. Each classroom also has a notebook for parents where they can leave notes for the teachers. Check your child's cubby daily for work to go home and for information that is posted for you.

We believe that parent conferences support communication. Upon enrollment, your classroom teacher will schedule a "Getting to Know You" conference. This conference is designed to find out about your child, family, routines, traditions, and at-home strategies. In this way we can aid in your child's transition to school and can support your child's learning style. In January, we have a winter check-in. This is a time when we check in with families and let you know briefly how your child is doing at school. In the spring, we prepare for a more in-depth conference. This is a chance for the teachers to share information they have gathered about your child's development using our assessment tool, the High/Scope Child Observation Record (COR). Additionally, you are welcome and encouraged to ask for a conference with teachers or our directors at any time during the year. Teachers are encouraged to request additional conferences with parents to discuss strategies for addressing any concerns about the child.

Essential Feature 6: Staff Training and Professional Development

Early childhood behavior-guidance policies should indicate a commitment to providing ongoing staff training and professional development regarding how to implement the guidance policy.

It is critical that programs ensure that staff have access to training and technical assistance in implementing policy guidelines and promoting the social competence of young children (Council for Children with Behavior Disorders, 2002; McEvoy and Welker,

2000; Strain and Joseph, 2004). Continued in-service training is necessary for building a sense of identity with and commitment to a program guidance policy. Fox and colleagues (2011) found a functional relationship between training and coaching of teachers and the implementation of practices associated with tiered models of intervention. Workforce development is a critical aspect of ensuring that evidence-based practices are implemented in the classroom (IOM and NRC, 2012), and continued opportunities for improving knowledge about evidence-based, developmentally appropriate practices (DAP) for promoting social and academic success are essential for all those who interact with and teach children.

For example, if the administrator knows that there are several students in the program who have developmental delays in communication, she may organize training to teach the staff communication accommodations and strategies such as pictorial schedules.

An example of an excerpt from a guidance policy that reflects Essential Feature 6 is provided below. Note that the policy commits to a minimum number of trainings within a given time period.

Sample Policy Statement Reflecting Essential Feature 6

The Children's Center believes that ongoing professional development for teachers is key to the success of the guidance policy. All staff and families are provided with a copy of the guidance policy at orientation, and staff are provided with a brief training on the guidance policy upon hire. In addition to the initial training, we provide ongoing professional-development workshops on evidence-based behavior-guidance practices that are promoted in the policy, such as positive behavior-support tiers. We require all staff to participate in a minimum of three professional-development workshops on behavior per year. The focus on teacher training is to ensure that teachers understand and know how to implement the practices in the guidance policy.

Essential Feature 7: Use of Data for Continuous Improvement

Early childhood behavior-guidance policies should reference the use of a data-collection system by which the relative success or failure of the behavior-guidance policy will be evaluated.

Finally, effective behavior-guidance policies should have demonstrable benefits, and the evaluation of a system-level guidance policy is necessary to determine if the policy is effective or in need of improvement (Sugai and Horner, 2002; Washburn, Burrello, and Buckmann, 2001). To do so, programs must establish structures, routines, and procedures for obtaining and using the data.

Fortunately, many forms of data, including incident reports, numbers of contacts and parent conferences concerning challenging behavior, types of violations of behavioral expectations, and the numbers of suspensions and expulsions, are naturally available to assist in the evaluation of policy effectiveness. Combined with the use of the TAGPEC, the use of data such as these will help programs

identify whether their policy is working and will support them to engage in a cycle of continuous improvement.

Sarah recently took part in a meeting with a Head Start director and her team in which they reflected on the effectiveness of their revised policy for supporting children with challenging behaviors. By using data regularly collected as part of program requirements, they realized that the number of referrals for outside mental-health consultation had dropped significantly from the previous year. In addition, they discussed how their focus on providing professional development related to the primary, preventative strategies described in Essential Feature 2 contributed to changes in classroom practices.

As we discussed in chapter three, our implicit biases, or the unconscious beliefs and stereotypes that we hold, affect our daily decisions about how we discipline children. Because we approach discipline from a humanistic perspective, we believe that we need more work acknowledging and addressing our implicit biases through professional development. One of the goals of Essential Feature 7 is to support programs in enacting policies that support early childhood staff in engaging in implicit-bias training and reflection.

Below is an example of an excerpt from a guidance policy that reflects Essential Feature 7. The policy statement emphasizes the families' involvement in guiding children's behavior as well as the need for specific types of professional-development training. Note that the statement identifies in the policy the types of data that the program collects and how often the data will be reviewed.

Sample Policy Statement Reflecting Essential Feature 7

Individual Child: Teachers and families are asked to document evidence of recurring challenging behaviors (the Children's Center provides easy-to-use behavior checklists) as well as efforts to use strategies, such as reinforcement charts and behavior checklists, to address challenging behaviors. The goal is to document progress of the child in improving his or her behavior and to revise the intervention strategies accordingly.

Teachers: Teachers are required to participate in ongoing professional development at least three times per year on topics related to effectively addressing challenging behaviors. Data will include training attendance sheets, training surveys, and training materials. A review of the training data will occur a minimum of once annually. Based on the data, the administrator will make recommendations for the following year's trainings.

Classroom/Program: Administrators will collect and review multiple forms of data to evaluate the effectiveness of the policy. Data may include referrals to director, referrals to community services, incident reports, behavior reports, the number of parent conferences, and the number of suspensions and expulsions. A review of the behavior-related data will occur a minimum of once annually. Based on the data, the administrator will make recommendations for improved guidance practices, revisions in policy language, teacher professional development, and improved data-collection strategies for the following year.

Conclusion

This chapter describes the research behind the seven essential features of guidance policies known to promote prosocial behavior, reduce challenging behaviors, and create social climates conducive to the academic success of young children. These features have been incorporated into The Teaching and Guidance Policy Essential Checklist discussed in chapter one. Using the TAGPEC, early childhood leaders are encouraged to reflect on their program-guidance policies and to initiate change, as needed.

We recommend pausing at this point and reviewing your program's existing guidance policy before moving on to the next chapter. Doing so will help leaders begin to think about how their policy aligns with the essential features. In the next chapter, we dive into the details regarding the structure and scoring of the TAGPEC. We will begin to explore how the TAGPEC can be used as a blueprint to help build an infrastructure that supports the children, families, and staff in your program.

The Structure and
Scoring of the TAGPEC

The purpose of this chapter is to provide early childhood program leaders with detailed information about the structure and scoring of the TAGPEC. Our goal is to help you better understand the various components of the tool. By the end of this chapter, you will be able to analyze the quality of existing policy statements using the TAGPEC as a guide. For those programs that don't yet have a standalone behavior-guidance policy, this chapter will assist leaders in better understanding the key components of a high-quality guidance policy.

The Structure of the TAGPEC

The TAGPEC is structured into three parts: essential features, items, and exemplar statements. The seven essential features represent the broad topic areas that we have identified as being essential for inclusion in a high-quality guidance policy. Each essential feature includes specific items, each of which defines specific criteria within that essential feature. Collectively, these thirty items assess the extent to which guidance policies are effectively supporting young children's social and emotional development and a positive classroom climate.

We've included exemplar statements for each essential feature to assist evaluators in identifying and crafting language to use in their guidance policy. These statements are meant to provide an example of how policy language can be written. However, we strongly encourage staff to work collaboratively to craft policy language that reflects the program's unique mission and goals. For example, consider how both of the statements below are written differently and yet still convey the essence of Essential Feature 1 on the intentional teaching of social-emotional skills.

Sample 1: Essential Feature 1 Policy Excerpt

When children receive positive, nonviolent, and understanding interactions from adults and others, they develop good self-concepts, problem-solving abilities, and self-discipline. The teacher is the primary guide for teaching children positive, nonviolent behavior in the classroom. Praise and positive reinforcement are effective methods of the behavior guidance of children. We use the strategies of positive behavior support to guide children with varying levels of social and emotional needs. These strategies include building relationships; establishing clear rules and routines; and teaching children emotional literacy, friendship, and anger-management skills.

Sample 2: Essential Feature 1 Policy Excerpt

Within the context of nurturing relationships, we support children in becoming self-disciplined. Becoming self-disciplined is a long-term process, and one of the major tasks in an early childhood classroom is assisting children with this process. At the Child Development Center, we are committed to supporting each child's progress toward becoming independent and self-disciplined. In practice, we provide an environment that encourages children to make choices and decisions, with a limited number of rules. We promote freedom within our environment as long as children do not disrupt the classroom or disregard the few rules that we do have. We help the children to quickly learn our routines and expectations while assisting them in developing ownership of these few rules.

Generally, children need guidance in using materials and interacting with others. At the Child Development Center, if a child continues to use materials inappropriately even after having been asked , that child is asked to find something else to do. This logical consequence is a clear reminder to children that materials have appropriate uses. If two children are in a conflict, they are encouraged to negotiate and discuss alternatives to solve the conflict peacefully. In some cases, this requires a great deal of teacher support and modeling. With practice, children can become independent in conflict resolution. In instances where children are repeatedly disruptive, out of control, or injuring themselves or others, they are removed from the group for the short time it takes for them to be calm enough to discuss alternate behaviors. They are then assisted in rejoining the group.

Note that the language is quite different in each of the two excerpts, reflecting the individual philosophies of the two programs. Nevertheless, both excerpts have clear evidence of including language essential to this feature, such as teaching social-emotional skills and positive teacher-child interactions. We encourage you to check this for yourself by re-reading the two excerpts, this time evaluating whether there is evidence that all four of the items in the essential feature are present.

Essential Feature 1: Intentional Focus on Teaching Social-Emotional Skills

Early childhood behavior-guidance policies should reflect an instructional, proactive approach to behavior guidance that supports the learning and practice of appropriate prosocial behavior of all children, regardless of individual differences and/or cultural and linguistic background.

Item 1: The policy clearly states that the goal of behavior guidance is to teach social-emotional skills to all children.

☐ Yes ☐ Emerging ☐ No

Item 2: The policy clearly describes the role of the teacher in proactively teaching all children social-emotional skills.

☐ Yes ☐ Emerging ☐ No

Item 3: The policy clearly describes the role of positive and consistent interactions among teachers and children in promoting positive behavior.

☐ Yes ☐ Emerging ☐ No

Item 4: Multiple evidence-based and developmentally appropriate strategies are described.

☐ Yes ☐ Emerging ☐ No

Hopefully you were able to identify language within each of the policy excerpts that shows how the policy addresses the items, albeit in different ways. For example, both present evidence of using multiple developmentally appropriate guidance strategies in their programs, but the specific strategies vary. For example, one uses praise and positive reinforcement, and the other emphasizes logical consequences. In summary, there are many ways to write a policy statement; what matters is that the policy conveys the fundamental principles inherent in each essential feature.

The following information provides a visual of how the TAGPEC is organized. Each component of the TAGPEC—the essential features, items, item descriptions, and exemplar statements—are labeled and briefly defined.

Table 6: The Organization of the TAGPEC

Essential Features and Items	Exemplar Statements
1. Intentional Focus on Teaching Social-Emotional Skills Early childhood behavior-guidance policies should reflect an instructional, proactive approach to behavior guidance that supports the learning and practice of appropriate prosocial behavior of all children, regardless of individual differences and/or cultural and linguistic backgrounds. • **Item 1:** The policy clearly states that the goal of behavior guidance is to teach social-emotional skills to all children. • **Item 2:** The policy clearly describes the role of the teacher in proactively teaching all children social-emotional skills. • **Item 3:** The policy clearly describes the role of positive and consistent interactions among teachers and children in promoting positive behavior. • **Item 4:** Multiple, evidence-based, developmentally appropriate strategies are described.	One of the goals of the Children's Center program is to assist children in learning to guide their own behavior. The role of the teacher is to help children learn to eventually solve their own problems and to provide children with the tools to do so. Additional strategies that are used to promote children's learning of positive behavior include: • Building relationships with children, families, and colleagues • Designing engaging environments • Establishing consistent and developmentally appropriate rules and routines • Implementing developmentally and culturally appropriate learning activities and providing feedback and encouragement • Modifying and adapting materials and activities to meet the individual needs of children
2. Developmentally and Culturally Appropriate Learning Environment Early childhood behavior-guidance policies should describe the importance of a developmentally appropriate learning environment that is predictable, engaging, and relationship based. • **Item 5:** The policy clearly describes the importance of nurturing and responsive teacher-child relationships as essential to preventing challenging behaviors. • **Item 6:** The policy emphasizes the importance of sufficient and active adult supervision of all children. • **Item 7:** The policy describes the need for staff to continuously (at all times) monitor and respond to children's behavior. • **Item 8:** The policy clearly describes the use of ecological arrangements, such as classroom environment and materials, as a means for promoting positive, prosocial behavior. • **Item 9:** The policy clearly describes the need for a predictable, intentional, and developmentally appropriate daily schedule; for example, including small and large group times, carefully planned transitions, and child- and adult-initiated activities. • **Item 10:** The policy clearly describes the value of an engaging curriculum as a deterrent to challenging behavior.	Our staff use a positive-guidance approach, which enables a child to develop self-control and assume responsibility for his or her own behavior. We stress the importance of establishing and fostering positive relationships between staff and children. We foster and guide a child's choices so his or her behavior will reflect peaceful human relationships with other children and adults. We provide an age-appropriate environment and curriculum that is stimulating, and we carefully consider how to use children's cultural and linguistic backgrounds to engage the children in meaningful activities conducive to the development of a positive self-image in each child. We believe in following a simple yet consistent set of developmentally appropriate rules so that children can thrive in a predictable and secure environment.

The Structure and Scoring of the TAGPEC

Table 6: The Organization of the TAGPEC

Essential Features and Items	Exemplar Statements
3. Setting Behavioral Expectations Early childhood behavior-guidance policies should describe clear and consistent expectations for behavior. • **Item 11:** The policy has clearly stated program-wide behavioral expectations that are developmentally appropriate and reflect the natural learning abilities typically associated with the age groups of children served. If this item is answered no, items 12–15 must be answered no as well. • **Item 12:** Behavioral expectations are stated positively and emphasize what children can and should do rather than what they cannot or should not do. • **Item 13:** Behavioral expectations are designed to promote children's self-regulation, promoting external to internal foci from staff to self. • **Item 14:** The policy describes the need for clearly defined rules that are observable and measurable at the classroom level. • **Item 15:** The policy describes the need for a connection between program-level behavioral expectations and classroom rules. • **Item 16:** The policy clearly describes practices that are unacceptable for use by staff, such as humiliation or depriving meals, snacks, rest, and so on.	Each class uses the same basic rules, which are as follows: 1 We keep ourselves safe. (We listen to the teacher; we stay with the group.) 2 We keep each other safe. (We use safe touches; we listen to one another.) 3 We keep our things safe.

4. Preventing and Addressing Challenging Behaviors Using a Tiered Model of Intervention

Early childhood behavior-guidance policies should identify primary, secondary, and tertiary preventative and intervention practices for promoting prosocial behavior and reducing challenging behavior in young children.

• **Item 17:** Procedures are in place to screen children for behavioral concerns.

• **Item 18:** The policy clearly describes the need to understand challenging behavior as children's efforts to communicate.

• **Item 19:** The policy clearly describes primary strategies to teach and reinforce prosocial behaviors in all children. (See Items 1–10.)

• **Item 20:** The policy describes targeted secondary strategies, such as the use of social-skills curricula and intentional small-group instruction, for children who are at risk for problem behaviors.

• **Item 21:** The policy clearly describes the use of tertiary strategies, such as developing a behavior support plan and early childhood mental-health consultation, for helping children who exhibit chronic and intense problem behaviors.

The Children's Program will use three curriculum models in their classrooms as a way to introduce and teach positive social skills. These curricula are *Pretend Public Schools Preschool Child Outcomes, Second Step,* and *Talking about Touching.* Each of these curricula emphasizes safety and the importance of understanding how someone else feels. They teach children to recognize the feelings of others and themselves, to solve their own problems, and to express their anger in nonviolent ways. Each curriculum emphasizes having the children practice and role play problem situations to use them in everyday interactions.

Table 6: The Organization of the TAGPEC

Essential Features and Items	Exemplar Statements
5. Working with Families Early childhood behavior-guidance policies should reflect the family-centered nature of early childhood education. • **Item 22:** The policy promotes proactive, rather than reactive, collaborative relationships as a means of promoting social competence in children. • **Item 23:** The policy promotes authentic staff-family collaboration in effectively dealing with challenging behavior, and families are given an opportunity to participate in developing and implementing interventions. • **Item 24:** The policy describes the need for obtaining contextually and culturally relevant information, such as at-home sleeping and eating habits, family events, and favorite toys and activities, from families in order to understand children's inappropriate behavior. • **Item 25:** The policy promotes embedding individual behavior-support-plan goals and objectives into family/home routines and activities.	The mission of the Children's Center is to provide developmentally appropriate, curriculum-based child care programs in a nurturing, loving, safe and stimulating environment. **We believe that parents are the primary educators of the child.** The home is the child's first and continual learning environment. Children come to school with different life experiences and skills that we acknowledge and draw upon as we plan for and facilitate new learning. Parents have an in-depth knowledge of their children. When parents share this knowledge, teachers can better understand each child. **We believe that parents are our partners.** We recognize that a child's home is the first and most important place of learning. Any information you give us concerning your family culture, rituals, or challenges helps us better understand your child's needs. By becoming involved with the classroom, you are supporting our philosophy of partnership and making a link between home and school. We invite your involvement in the classroom by helping out with a special activity, an ongoing activity, and/or on field trips. **We believe that communication is key.** Communication on all levels is important. Families receive program and classroom-specific newsletters at least quarterly. Upcoming events and activities are posted by the front door and on each classroom's bulletin board. Teachers make an effort to talk with each child's parent at least once a day. Each classroom also has a notebook where parents can leave notes for the teachers. Check your child's cubby daily for work to go home and for information that is posted for you. **We believe that parent conferences support communication.** Upon enrollment, your classroom teacher will schedule a "Getting to Know You" conference. This conference is designed to find out about your child, family, routines, traditions, and at-home strategies. In this way we can aid in your child's transition to school and can support his or her learning style. In January, we have a winter check-in. This is a time when we check in with families and let you know briefly how your child is doing at school. In the spring, we prepare for a more in-depth conference. This is a chance for the teachers to share information they have gathered about your child's development using our assessment tool, the *High/Scope Child Observation Record* (COR). You are welcomed and encouraged to ask for a conference with teachers or our directors at any time during the year. Teachers are encouraged to request additional conferences with parents to discuss strategies for addressing concerns with the child.

The Structure and Scoring of the TAGPEC

Table 6: The Organization of the TAGPEC

Essential Features and Items	Exemplar Statements

6. Staff Training and Professional Development

Early childhood behavior-guidance policies should indicate a commitment to providing ongoing staff training and professional development regarding how to implement the guidance policy.

- **Item 26:** The policy describes practices that are in place to ensure that staff understand and can articulate the behavior-guidance policy.

- **Item 27:** The policy describes a process for ongoing professional-development opportunities to support staff in the use of evidence-based prevention and intervention strategies.

- **Item 28:** The policy describes the intent of the program to ensure that staff have a strong understanding of culture and diversity and are provided opportunities to engage in self-reflection and ongoing professional development that encourage awareness of implicit and explicit biases that may affect their work with children and families.

The Children's Center believes that ongoing professional development for teachers is key to the success of the guidance policy. All staff and families are provided with a copy of the guidance policy at orientation, and staff are provided with a brief training on the guidance policy upon hire. In addition to the initial training, we provide ongoing professional-development workshops on evidence-based behavior-guidance practices that are promoted in the policy. We require all staff to participate in a minimum of three professional-development workshops on behavior per year. The focus on teacher training is to ensure that teachers understand and know how to implement the practices in the guidance policy.

7. Use of Data for Continuous Improvement

Early childhood behavior-guidance policies should reference the use of a data-collection system by which the relative success or failure of the behavior-guidance policy will be evaluated.

- **Item 29:** Policy-evaluation procedures are in place and clearly describe how the success or failure of the policy will be measured.

- **Item 30:** The policy describes how data will be used to engage in continuous improvement to ensure that practices are in line with the intent of the behavior-guidance policy and to ensure fairness and equity for all children.

Individual Child: Teachers and families are asked to document evidence of recurring challenging behaviors (the Children's Center provides easy-to-use behavior checklists) as well as efforts to use strategies, such as reinforcement charts and behavior checklists, to address challenging behaviors. The goal is to document progress of the child in improving his or her behavior and to revise the intervention strategies accordingly.

Classroom/Program: Administrators will collect and review multiple forms of data to evaluate the effectiveness of the policy. Data may include referrals to the director, referrals to community services, incident reports, behavior reports, the number of parent conferences, and the number of suspensions and expulsions. A review of the behavior-related data will occur a minimum of once per year. Based on the data, the administrator will make recommendations for the following year for improved guidance practices, revisions in policy language, teacher professional development, and improved data-collection strategies.

Scoring the TAGPEC

Administrators can use the TAGPEC to quickly evaluate the quality of their program's guidance policy. On average, it takes only twenty to twenty-five minutes to administer and score the TAGPEC. To score, evaluators rate each item according to three dimensions: Yes, Emerging, or No. Evaluators respond yes when there is clear evidence of the essential feature in the behavior-guidance policy. Select emerging when there is some but not clear evidence of the essential feature in the behavior-guidance policy. Select no when there is little or no evidence of the essential feature in the behavior-guidance policy. Each dimension gets a different score, such that *Yes* equals two points, *Emerging* equals one point, and

No equals zero points. When the evaluator has completed the scoring, she sums the total number of responses, resulting in a total score out of a possible sixty points. This total score is recorded into the scoring section of the TAGPEC. Figure 5 shows a sample completed TAGPEC scoring sheet.

We've created an online scoring sheet, which can be completed by any team member who is familiar with Excel. The self-scoring template can be easily downloaded from the TAGPEC website under the tab Administration and Scoring. Alternatively, the TAGPEC is simple enough to be scored by hand, as is shown in the figure below.

Figure 5: Sample Scored TAGPEC

Scoring

Steps

Step 1: Calculate the score total.

• No = 0 • Emerging = 1 • Yes = 2

Step 2: Sum all of the item scores to get a total score.

Step 3: Enter essential feature scores in the summary section.

Step 4: Enter the total score in the summary section.

Step 5: Higher item scores are strengths.

Summary Section

Essential Feature	Subscale/Total Score	# of Items	Average Score
1: Intentional Teaching Approach	2	÷ 4	= .50
2: Developmentally Appropriate Learning Environment	4	÷ 6	= .67
3: Clear and Developmentally Appropriate Learning Expectations	4	÷ 6	= .67
4: Tiered Model of Intervention	3	÷ 5	= .60
5: Working with Families	2	÷ 4	= .50
6: Staff Training and Professional Development	1	÷ 3	= .33
7: Data Monitoring and Improvement	1	÷ 2	= .50
TOTAL	17	÷ 30	= .57

Comments Section

Policy Strengths: Clear, developmentally appropriate learning expectations, but need more info on multiple strategies used; discuss importance of environment and curriculum in behavior. Strong at Tier 1.

Policy Areas for Improvement: Need to mention teaching approach in policy statement. Little information on how families are involved when behavior becomes a chronic problem; little information on staff training and data monitoring. Need more information for Tiers 2 and 3.

Scoring Emerging Policy Statements

When scoring policies, it can be difficult at times to discern the difference between a statement that is emerging and a statement that qualifies as a yes. The excerpt below is a good example. Read it, and then score it according to TAGPEC Item 4: Multiple, evidence-based, developmentally appropriate strategies are described.

In taking disciplinary action, the teacher considers what is most appropriate for a particular situation and the children involved. The outcome should be to resolve the conflict as well as empower the children to gain self-awareness and problem-solving skills. Our teachers will use one of the following strategies:

- Resolution of conflict: Clarify what happened and how each person is feeling. Then, question and examine possible solutions with the children.

- Note: Feelings—both children's and adults'—are an important part of life, requiring attention and expression. We encourage and support open and direct communication. We believe that both positive and negative feelings are real and valid and that school should be a safe place to explore them.

- Redirection: When a child is unable to behave appropriately in certain areas, with certain children or toys, the teacher may ask the child to play in a different area until he or she is able to behave appropriately.

- Separation from group: This is sometimes needed when a child cannot regain self-control. The teacher acknowledges the purpose of separation: regaining self-control, calming down, and so on. The child is with the teacher—not sent to time-out—only long enough to regain self-control. The teacher may say something like, "Let me know when you are ready to try again."

In light of Item 4, what did you score this policy? Since there was some evidence of the use of developmentally appropriate strategies, we scored it as a 1 for Emerging. Had there been additional strategies listed, then it would be scored a 2 for yes. We like to think of 2 as the ideal because it guides teacher practice; therefore, we suggest scoring an item a 2 only when there is substantial evidence for it. One simple test for this is to have several teachers review the policy and to ask them whether the information is clear enough for them to be able to implement it in the classroom.

Interpreting the Results of the TAGPEC

In general, the higher the score on the TAGPEC, the more the policy integrates the essential features known to promote positive social and emotional adjustment in young children. The highest possible score on the TAGPEC is 60. If a policy scores 30 points, for example, then it contains exactly half of those features known to be best practice in promoting positive behavior guidance. Recall that most of the policies that we have scored in our research scored, on average, under this halfway mark.

Although formal benchmarks for the TAGPEC have not been established, the guidelines below may provide a useful way for evaluators to interpret the total TAGPEC score.

Guidelines for Interpreting Total TAGPEC Score

Total average score is a .90 or above: Excellent

Behavior-guidance policy clearly and thoroughly describes the use of developmentally appropriate, evidence-based guidance practices. The policy captures items from most if not all of the essential features.

Total score is .80–.89: Good

Behavior-guidance policy provides a clear description of the use of developmentally appropriate, evidence-based guidance practices. Some details are provided regarding how teachers promote positive behavior in the classroom.

Total score is .70–.79: Adequate

Behavior-guidance policy provides an adequate description of the use of developmentally appropriate, evidence-based guidance practices.

Total score is .60–.69: Minimal

Behavior-guidance policy provides a minimum description of the use of developmentally appropriate, evidence-based guidance practices.

Total score is .50–.59 or below: Inadequate

Behavior-guidance policy does not sufficiently describe the use of developmentally appropriate, evidence-based guidance practices.

By way of example, Figure 5 shows a final average total score of .57 out of a total possible average score of 1.0. A score of .57, when interpreted through the scale above, would be categorized as inadequate. This score means that the program has some elements of what is known to be essential for guidance policies but is missing key components. It is important to note which items are not addressed in the policy and to consider ways of integrating them, because ultimately it is policy that guides practice.

Evaluators are also asked to write comments in the scoring section regarding policy strengths and areas for improvement. We suggest examining scores on individual items to help guide the completion of the comments section. For instance, if a policy was scored as a 0 on Item 27: The policy describes a process for ongoing professional-development opportunities to support staff in the use of evidence-based prevention and intervention strategies, then the evaluator could make a note in the areas to improve

section such as, "Include the number and type of annual mandated professional trainings on behavior guidance in the policy." A sample of a completed TAGPEC scoring form is provided in the appendix.

In sum, the TAGPEC can be an excellent tool for assessing the quality of an early childhood program behavior-guidance policy. In this chapter, we have given an overview of the structure of the TAGPEC. Each of the components provides valuable information for guiding program leaders through the process of conducting a self-assessment of their behavior-guidance policy.

In the next chapter, we describe a simple five-step process for how early childhood program leaders can improve their own behavior-guidance policies. By the end of the next chapter, you will be well on your way to having a behavior-guidance policy that will serve as a blueprint for supporting the social, emotional, and academic success of all children in your program.

The Structure and Scoring of the TAGPEC

How to Use the TAGPEC to Guide Policy Improvement:
A Simple, Five-Step Process

The TAGPEC can be an excellent tool for assessing and improving the quality of early childhood program behavior-guidance policies. In this chapter, we describe how you can use the TAGPEC to guide policy-improvement efforts. Whether you are developing a new guidance policy or improving an existing one, the TAGPEC provides an excellent blueprint for guiding the process.

We have broken the policy-improvement process into five simple steps, each of which is explained and illustrated with examples from case studies.

Five Steps to Improving Your Behavior-Guidance Policy

Step 1: Assemble your behavior-guidance team.

Step 2: Commit to improving your behavior-guidance policy and practice.

Step 3: Collect the program guidance policy and practice documents.

Step 4: Assess the quality of your behavior-guidance policy using the TAGPEC.

Step 5: Implement and monitor your action plan to improve your behavior-guidance policy.

Before diving into the steps of policy improvement, we'd like to talk briefly about the critical role of the early childhood leader in guiding the policy-improvement process. As administrators, leaders are uniquely poised to influence behavior change at the program policy level. We believe that leaders who go into the policy-improvement process with a committed, collaborative, and creative mind-set are strongly positioned to be successful in reforming their guidance policies.

The Role of Leadership in Guiding Policy-Improvement Efforts

Effective leadership is widely recognized as playing a pivotal role in the success of early childhood education programs. Leaders in the early childhood setting are most often program administrators or principals but may also be supervisors, teachers, counselors, or parent liaisons, among others. When early childhood program leaders commit to the process of monitoring, assessing, and improving their program in ways that align with best practices, everyone benefits, including children, families, teachers, and the administrators themselves. Recent studies examining the influence of early childhood leaders on program quality show a consistent link between effective leadership, child outcomes, and educational equity (Leithwood et al., 2006; Mitgang, 2012).

But, what is it that makes early childhood leader effective, specifically in the area of program-improvement efforts? In this section, we summarize the underlying qualities that effective early childhood leaders possess. We focus on three qualities known to support program-improvement processes in meaningful and sustainable ways. These three qualities are commitment, collaboration, and creativity.

Commitment

Effective early childhood leaders are committed to the underlying cause of the improvement effort. The cause is the "so what?" question that guides the future work. In the case of behavior-guidance policies, the "so what" question might be, "So what if we change our behavior-guidance policy. How will that improve the teachers' practices and the children's outcomes?"

One possible response is, "By improving our behavior-guidance policy, we are articulating concrete commitments and guidelines for young children's behavior and well-being. Our policy, which is founded on evidence-based practices, guides teachers and families toward using evidence-based practices and reduces the likelihood of problem behavior in children."

An additional "so what" question might relate to the issue of inequity of discipline practices in early childhood education: "How will improving our behavior-guidance policy help us to ensure that our guidance practices are fair for all children in our program? The response could be, "Our behavior-guidance policy will address inequity by providing clear procedures for how all children are guided and by making a commitment to monitoring and assessing behavior-guidance practices on an ongoing basis." When leaders commit to strong position statements about practices that matter to them, it makes it easier for everyone to invest—and stay invested—in the process.

Collaboration

Regardless of how committed and effective an early childhood leader is, she needs the support of teachers and families to carry out a collective vision for behavior support. Genuine buy-in and support is especially critical when talking about behavior guidance, because teachers and family members are the ones who are engaging in a majority of the practices outlined in the behavior-guidance policy. For example, teachers are most often the ones at school who are responsible for teaching children appropriate behavioral expectations. It makes sense, then, that teachers would have an opportunity to

participate in developing the policy, including forming goals for the improvement of practices related to behavior guidance and teaching social and emotional skills.

Collaboration begins with everyone coming to a shared understanding of the goals of the behavior-guidance policy. Details about how to set up a collaboration, as well as guiding questions to facilitate this process, are included later in this chapter. For now, the main idea is that it is critical to engage others in the process early enough so that the policy is grounded in clearly defined and shared goals for children's behavior.

Creativity

Whether you are revising an existing behavior-guidance policy or designing a new one, the process requires that leaders be creative. In our experience, behavior-guidance policies are often written to conform to state licensing standards, which tend to focus on

children's health and safety but not as much on their social and emotional development. Truly changing behavior practices in an early childhood program takes innovation. There are many ways that leaders can be innovative in how they design their guidance policy. For example, leaders are creative when they seek new knowledge about behavior guidance and incorporate this knowledge into the policy. Leaders are creative when they introduce a new assessment into the program for how behavior problems will be measured or when they design new strategies for partnering with families around children's problem behaviors.

There is no one "right" way to design a behavior-guidance policy, which opens many opportunities for creative thinking. Your behavior-guidance policy can capture the essential features of a high-quality guidance policy and still reflect your program's specific vision for children's early education and care. We provide several examples of high-quality behavior-guidance policies in appendix C, which show a variety of ways policies can be written.

In sum, leaders are integral to the success of a behavior-guidance policy. While the program administrator is often in an ideal position to serve as the leader in facilitating behavior policy change, others, such as teachers and parent liaisons, can serve as leaders as well. The qualities of commitment, collaboration, and creativity can be extremely helpful in assuring that a leader is successful when reforming their guidance policy.

Five Steps to Improving Your Behavior-Guidance Policy

In this section, we outline the five simple steps that leaders can follow to design or redesign their guidance policy. Each step is accompanied by supplemental, optional resources to assist evaluators in moving through the process with efficiency and effectiveness. A majority of these resources are contained within the TAGPEC workbook, which can be found in the appendix on page 127. Additional resources, including scoring templates and technical support, are located on our website: http://go.sdsu.edu/education/tagpec/.

Step 1: Assemble Your Behavior-Guidance Team

The first step in the process of writing or revising your behavior-guidance policy is to assemble your team. Consider inviting individuals who are willing and able to take ownership of the process and to connect with the goal of improving child behavior outcomes. We recommend that you seek participation from a range of individuals, including administrators, teachers, supervisors, support staff, parents, and early childhood mental health and early intervention staff. Ideally, you would have at least one member from each stakeholder group—administration, teachers, family, community—participate in the process.

To help program leaders get started with this step, we have included Worksheet 1: Building a Behavior-Guidance Team in the TAGPEC workbook on page 127. The goal with worksheet 1 is to help program leaders identify potential team members as well as their roles and responsibilities. The worksheet includes tips for team members to consider when planning the policy improvement process, including how to:

- Set the tone by defining the purpose of the team

- Define the community capacity of the team

- Identify potential barriers to success

- Formalize roles, procedures, and responsibilities

- Clarify the benefits and barriers of the process

By building your team, you are not only developing a support network for your behavior-guidance policy, but you are also taking the first step toward building an infrastructure that is systematic, intentional, and grounded in the belief that all children can be successful. Your infrastructure consists of those individuals who are not only committed to the success of each individual child in your program but also provide a real voice to the needs of those involved. These individuals are integral to designing and carrying out the behavior blueprint for your program.

Step 2: Commit to Improving Your Behavior-Guidance Policy and Practice

The process of (re)designing your behavior-guidance policy begins when the behavior-guidance team makes the commitment to improve the social, academic, and emotional success of all the children in the program. To make this commitment, the team will need to determine why this process is important to them. As we've shared in earlier chapters, there are many reasons why improving your policy can be good for your program: less challenging behavior, better-trained staff, more-involved families, fewer suspensions and expulsions, and fewer problems with inequity in how discipline is administered to children.

We recommend that you and your team begin by reviewing the underlying principles of the humanistic approach to behavior guidance. Reviewing these principles together can help to guide early conversations about the research on behavior guidance, as well as conversations about the teams' goals for how they want behavior guidance to improve in the program. For those team members who are especially interested in the research on challenging behaviors, we encourage you to share chapter 4 with them, as it provides more detail on evidence-based approaches.

A Humanistic Approach to Behavior Guidance

- The role of the adult is to teach children appropriate social-emotional skills.

- Relationships guide and regulate behaviors.

- Behavior is communication.

- Each child is a unique individual.

- Implicit bias affects decision making.

Because challenging behaviors always occur within the context of relationships, it is essential that team members reflect on their beliefs about behavior and, in particular, how their values, beliefs, and assumptions may contribute to or reinforce children's challenging behavior. As research shows, teachers' and parents' perspectives on discipline are deeply rooted in personal, cultural, and community values (Garrity, Shapiro, Longstreth, and Bailey, 2017). It is worthwhile to spend time as a team reflecting on and sharing these values and perspectives so that the team can come to a unified approach when designing the behavior-guidance policy.

Worksheet 2: Behavior-Guidance Team Reflection Questions on page 130 provides a set of discussion questions that teams can use to guide them through this phase of the process. At the end of the worksheet, you will be asked to work with your team to create a behavior-guidance commitment statement, which we recommend referring to throughout the process to maintain focus on the larger goal of supporting the social, emotional, and academic success of all children. Below is a

sample of a behavior-guidance commitment statement developed by one program.

A sample of a complete worksheet 2, which includes an additional sample behavior-guidance commitment statement, can be found on page 131. These samples demonstrate how multiple stakeholders can come together to write a unified position on behavior guidance.

Sample Behavior-Guidance Commitment Statement

We believe that all children have the potential to succeed emotionally, socially, and academically. We, the staff and families of Children's Center, are committed to promoting the success of all children. We believe we can do this by offering children a rich curriculum, supportive relationships with adults, and a comprehensive program of prevention and intervention strategies. Social-emotional learning is the foundation of children's academic success, and our staff and families are expected to take a role in nurturing children's prosocial skills.

Step 3: Collect the Program Guidance Policy and Practice Documents

Now that you and your team have developed a strong, clear behavior-guidance commitment statement, it is time to collect all of the existing information you have available in the program that relates to behavior guidance. The goal with step 3 is to gather information about the program so that you can compare the data to your newly written commitment statement. Ultimately, you want to make sure that your policies and practices are aligned.

Often, information about behavior guidance is embedded within broader program documents such as staff or parent handbooks. Less frequently, programs will have an existing stand-alone behavior-guidance policy. Additional sources of information on child behavior in your program may be located in the following places:

- Licensing documents

- Parent handbook

- Parent communication, such as newsletters

- Staff handbook

- Photos and documents, such as visual schedules and clearly posted behavioral expectations, from classrooms that demonstrate the use of primary prevention practices

- Incident report forms

- Behavior-support-plan forms

- Referral forms

- Family communication about problem behavior

- Behavior data-collection tools, such as behavior observation forms

This list is not meant to be exhaustive; indeed, evidence of behavior-guidance practices may be integrated throughout various documents and artifacts. The key is to search for all of the information that you currently have so that you can consider what it says about your program's current approach to behavior guidance.

Once you have collected all of the available documents on behavior guidance within your program, it is time for you and your team to evaluate each item in relation to your newly developed commitment statement. To do this, we suggest laying all of the physical documents on a large table and then going through them, one by one, asking the question, "How does this document support our belief and commitment to positive behavior guidance?" Refer to your completed worksheet 2 from step 2 to remind your team of your commitment statement. Then, refer to Worksheet 3: Behavior-Guidance Document Checklist on page 132. List the type document reviewed in the first column and, in the second column, check whether or not the document fulfills an important element of your commitment statement. Use the third column to make notes about what is working and what is still needed for each of the documents.

One of the most important parts of this process is to determine whether your program is sending a consistent message that reflects your commitment statement. Does the information provided to staff in the staff manual reflect what is in the parent handbook? Is this information consistent with your referral

process? See the completed worksheet 3 on page 133 as an example of how this form can be completed. Note that the worksheet gives the team a place to jot down areas in which more information about behavior is needed or where there are discrepancies between the existing documents and the new commitment statement.

As a final note regarding the data-collection phase, we recommend that you systematically organize all of the documents that you've collected thus far into a hardcopy or electronic folder with a label such as "Behavior-Guidance Policy." These documents will be important to have readily available when it comes time to consider how you will integrate the language of the policy into all relevant program documentation. For instance, after you have finalized your behavior-guidance policy, you will most likely need to update sections of your parent and staff handbooks to include similar language.

Next, store all of the documents you've collected, keeping out only that single document that most comprehensively articulates your existing guidance policy. For most programs, this will be the guidance or discipline section of the parent handbook, but it could also be a separate document. If you have not yet developed a section or a document specific to behavior guidance, then refer to the licensing regulations that are required by your state. Each state has a section in their regulations that addresses the topic of discipline. This core document will serve as your baseline for your first review using the TAGPEC.

It's now time for you and your team to evaluate the extent to which your commitment is aligned with your policies.

Step 4: Assess the Quality of Your Existing Behavior-Guidance Policy Using the TAGPEC

In step 1, you identified the team members who will be responsible for assessing your core guidance-policy document with the TAGPEC. We recommend that at least two team members conduct individual assessments using the TAGPEC and then come back together to discuss findings and come to a consensus on the items. Ideally, you will reach a consensus through a fair process such as voting or inviting additional reviewers to assess an item. If two team members aren't available, then one person can be the assessor and can report the results to the rest of the team. What is important is that the team members are ultimately able to come to an agreement about the final TAGPEC scores. Typically, this will mean that the assessors will bring any ambiguous items to the team for discussion and consensus before finalizing a score.

On our website at http://go.sdsu.edu/education/tagpec/, we offer a free and easy-to-use training webinar that shows evaluators how to administer and score the TAGPEC. We recommend that each team member serving as an assessor complete the online training. Assessors will receive a TAGPEC reliability training certificate upon successful completion of the training module.

For those teams who wish to score their policy on their own, we have made the checklist as easy as possible to use. As described in chapter 5, you will go through each of the thirty items and rate them using only the evidence within the core guidance policy document. If, for example, there is no information in your policy about behavior-support plans—even if you implement them in practice—then mark no for that item. Keep in mind that the purpose of this tool is not to judge or penalize a program for what is or isn't in its policy but rather to help a program make decisions about where change is needed and to take steps toward making sure that their guidance policy reflects a commitment to using evidence-based best practices. Chapter 5 has more detailed instructions for how to score and interpret your policy using the TAGPEC, as well as a sample of a scored TAGPEC.

Once the assessor has scored the TAGPEC, he will schedule a meeting with the team to report and discuss the results. If there were any items that the assessor had difficulty scoring, then this is the time to discuss them and come to a consensus.

We provide some general guidelines in chapter 4 on how to interpret the scores of the TAGPEC. For instance, we give criteria for low, mid, and high ranges, which may provide teams with a useful point of reference for interpreting the quality of the policy. It is important to note, however, that these cut points are only meant as a general guide. The most useful approach is to aim for a total higher score, since the higher the score, the better the quality of the policy.

We also recommend examining average scores within each essential feature, as well as item scores, as these can provide important insights about areas in which your policy is strong and areas that need improvement. For example, if a policy scores .80 out of 1.0 on Essential Feature 2, but only .25 out of 4.0 on Essential Feature 5, then it would make sense to prioritize the short-term goal of improving the items in Essential Feature 5 while keeping Essential Feature 2 in mind as a longer-term goal. The scoring sheet allows you to view the overall score of the policy as well as average scores and percentiles for each essential feature.

The final step in step 4 is to transfer the scores to the TAGPEC Worksheet 4: The Behavior-Guidance Policy Action Plan (page 134). The purpose of the action plan is to assist the team in developing goals for improving the guidance policy that are directly aligned with the data from the TAGPEC. In other words, teams will be asked to consider, with the evidence in hand, what aspects of the policy are strong and can be kept and what aspects of the policy need more information or need to be revised. The action plan also asks teams to consider both their short-term and long-term goals, to plan in a way that is realistic and attainable. Completing the action plan is a critical part of the process; therefore, we strongly recommend that it be completed with all team members present. The decisions that are made at this step will inform future decisions, including the allocation of resources, such as coaching and in-service trainings. Examples of short- and long-term action plan goals may include the following:

- **Short-term goal:** Within two months, we will change the policy to reflect our commitment to working with families as partners, especially when behavior problems arise. We will outline the steps in the policy for how chronic behavior problems will be addressed with the families. We will share the policy with families when they enroll in the program, and we will have them sign a copy and return it with their enrollment packets.

- **Long-term goal:** In twelve months, we will change the policy to reflect our commitment to providing staff with a minimum of three trainings on the topic of behavior guidance. This year, we will focus at least one professional-development training on the topic of partnering with families and one on addressing implicit biases in our guidance practices. The final training will be determined by the specific needs of the staff.

One strategy that many programs have found useful when writing goals for their action plans is to consider how the TAGPEC scores compare to other data that the program has collected on behavior guidance. We recommend, for example, simultaneously reviewing scores from the ITERS, ECERS, CLASS, and/or TPOT, if these scores are available. Each of these measures has items that correlate with TAGPEC items and therefore may be good sources for considering how the policy can be better implemented.

Now that your team has a clearly articulated behavior-guidance policy action plan, you are ready to move on to the final phase of the process: implementation.

Step 5: Implement and Monitor Your Action Plan to Improve Your Behavior-Guidance Policy

You have developed a clearly articulated action plan, and now you are ready to execute it. We suggest beginning this process by coming together again as a team and reviewing your commitment statement. Although this is the final stage in the process, it also requires a significant level of time and energy. It is important to ensure that everyone maintains a commitment to the original policy beliefs.

Begin by looking at your short-term goals. Consider, as a team, how working on those first will help to create change in your long-term goals. For example, one of your short-term goals may be to introduce clearer behavioral expectations throughout your program. This will, in the long-term, help you to work on your goal of providing regular staff professional development on behavior expectations. Go through each of your goals this same way, each time drafting new language that you might include in your revised policy. Pay attention to the language in the items of the TAGPEC, as it can help to guide you in crafting a statement that is founded in evidence-based practices.

There is no one right way to go through the process of drafting and revising a new policy document. Some teams may decide that they prefer to work together while they are drafting the policy; others might prefer to divide the goals among the team members and then share their ideas later. The process is unique to each program, but the important thing is that you write policy language that aligns with your commitment statement, your policy goals, and the evidence-based practices described in the TAGPEC.

The action plan has a section asking the team to determine which resources are needed to carry out the policy goals. The administrator can provide key information on what resources may be available in the program, community, or online. We've provided ideas for the types of goals and resources that programs might find useful in the tables on pages 80-81.

Once the policy is in a complete draft form, the entire team reviews and approves it for use in the program. The policy is then communicated to all key members of the program, including teachers and families.

Table 7: Sample Short-Term Goals and Resources

Short-Term Goals	Resources
Revise the guidance policy to reflect the mission to teach children social-emotional skills.	• Collaborative for Academic, Social, and Emotional Learning (CASEL): http://www.casel.org • Goleman, Daniel. 1995. *Emotional Intelligence: Why It Can Matter More than IQ.* New York: Bantam. • Lewin-Benham, Ann. 2015. *Eight Essential Techniques for Teaching with Intention.* New York: Teachers College Press/ St. Paul, MN: Redleaf
Revise the guidance policy to include program-wide behavior expectations.	Positive Behavioral Interventions and Supports (PBIS). School-Wide Positive Behavioral Interventions and Support for Beginners, https://www.pbis.org/school/swpbis-for-beginners
Revise the guidance policy to state that parents are considered partners at the beginning, not just when problems arise.	Harvard Family Research Project. Family Involvement Projects, http://www.hfrp.org/family-involvement/projects
Revise the guidance policy to indicate that all staff receive a copy of the policy and are trained on the policy as part of their hiring orientation.	Bergen, Sharon. 2016. *Early Childhood Staff Orientation Guide: Facilitator's Edition.* St. Paul, MN: Redleaf.

Table 8: Sample Long-Term Goals and Resources

Long-Term Goals	Resources
Revise the guidance policy to include more information on tier 2 and tier 3 interventions.	• The Division for Early Childhood of the Council for Exceptional Children (DEC), National Association for the Education of Young Children (NAEYC), and National Head Start Association (NHSA). 2013. "Frameworks for Response to Intervention in Early Childhood: Description and Implications." http://www.naeyc.org/files/naeyc/RTI%20in%20 Early%20Childhood.pdf • PBIS, Tier 2 Supports, https://www.pbis.org/ school/tier2supports • PBIS, Tier 3 Supports, https://www.pbis.org/ school/tier-3-supports
Revise the guidance policy to include a process for gathering contextual and cultural information from families about behavior and to define how this information can be used to partner with families when children have challenging behaviors.	• Technical Assistance Center on Social-Emotional Intervention (TACSEI), http://challengingbehavior. fmhi.usf.edu/communities/families.htm • Harvard Family Research Project, http://www. hfrp.org/family-involvement/projects
Revise the guidance policy to indicate the types and frequency of professional-development trainings to be offered to staff per year.	• NAEYC Professional Development Glossaries, https://www.naeyc.org/ecp • Bergen, Sharon. 2009. *Best Practices for Training Early Childhood Professionals.* St. Paul, MN: Redleaf.

Continued Monitoring of the Quality of the Behavior-Guidance Policy

We encourage you to meet periodically with your team to examine and evaluate the extent to which the behavior-guidance policy is improving teacher and child outcomes. For example, note increases in teachers' use of developmentally appropriate, evidence-based strategies and/or decreases in children's challenging behaviors. If a program makes significant revisions to the behavior policy but does not see an improvement in teachers' use of positive behavior-guidance strategies or in children's frequency of challenging behaviors, then that program might consider how it could improve its efforts to communicate the policy to staff and families. We suggest keeping ongoing, dated notes in your behavior-guidance folder about changes that you notice in the way the policy is inter-

preted and used by staff and families. Every few months, take time to analyze your notes for patterns relating to teachers' use of the policies in practice.

In summary, the TAGPEC can be a useful tool for assessing and improving the quality of early childhood program guidance policies. In this chapter, we described how early childhood professionals can use the TAGPEC to guide policy-improvement efforts. The TAGPEC Workbook on pages 127-136 has many resources useful for moving through each of the five steps effectively and efficiently. In the next and final chapter, we will explore the topic of trauma and its role in influencing child behavior and adjustment.

The Impact of Early Childhood Trauma on Children's Behavior and Adjustment

Jack is fourteen and is living in a temporary emergency shelter for displaced youth. Since he was two, Jack has been in the custody of the state, having been removed from his home after his parents were convicted of physically abusing him and his two older siblings. Over the last twelve years, he has lived in eight foster-care homes and three residential group homes. He has a history, beginning at age three, of aggressive behavior toward other children and adults. When he was four, he was suspended from preschool for tying up a classmate with a jump rope during recess and threatening to strangle her. By the time he was five, he had been expelled from two preschools and suspended for three days from kindergarten for violent behavior, including kicking a teacher in the leg and injuring her so severely that she required surgery. Jack's aggression, fueled by his deep-rooted fear of rejection, abuse, and abandonment, continued to escalate throughout his childhood until, ultimately, at age thirteen, he was arrested for vandalizing school property and assaulting a security guard. With a juvenile record and no family, Jack's social worker placed him in a temporary emergency shelter. This morning, the shelter had to call the police to come and arrest Jack. He, along with two other teens, is accused of beating a counselor at the shelter, nearly to death. The counselor, despite being critically injured, responded to the police with conflicting emotions—he wanted to help Jack. Helping kids was why he entered the profession. And yet, it felt like Jack had turned on the very person who was trying to help. The counselor didn't know what else to do at this point but to press charges. Jack was charged, and the police took him to juvenile hall.

Although extreme in nature, Jack's case illustrates the need to address persistent and severe challenging behavior more effectively in the early years. Decades of research in developmental science have shown us that programs that provide support to children with challenging behaviors are making a big impact in reducing the offenses of these youth later in life. When we look at Jack's case, we can see what can happen, in the extreme, when we don't offer these children access to the resources that we know can help them. As with Jack, a large majority of youth who are convicted of juvenile crimes started showing signs of these behaviors in early childhood (Sickmund and Puzzanchera, 2014). And, like Jack, their early years are characterized by poor academic perfor-

mance, peer rejection, and/or suspensions and expulsions.

There is a small but growing percentage of children who, like Jack, need intensive, comprehensive mental-health services that cannot always be provided in a typical early childhood setting. The purpose of this chapter is to summarize the research on the impact of early childhood trauma on children's behavior and adjustment. Because of the nature of trauma, most of the discussion in this chapter focuses on the child within the context of the family system. However, at the end of the chapter, we provide practical suggestions for how early childhood professionals can address trauma-related behaviors in both policy and practice.

What Is Trauma?

According to the National Institute of Mental Health, a traumatic event is defined as a "shocking, scary, or dangerous experience that affects someone emotionally" (https://

www.nimh.nih.gov/health/topics/coping-with-traumatic-events/index.shtml). These experiences can include natural disasters; accidents; bullying; a sudden and/or serious medical condition; violence in the home, school, or in the surrounding community; war or terrorism; and being a refugee. Trauma also includes chaos or dysfunction in the home, including domestic violence, a family member with a mental illness, an incarcerated parent, a family member with a substance-abuse problem, or the death of a loved one. Emotional abuse or neglect, physical abuse, sexual abuse, or separation from a parent or caregiver are also traumatic events, as is the stress caused by poverty.

Adverse Childhood Experiences

The Adverse Childhood Experiences (ACEs) study has been monumental in focusing attention on the effects of early childhood trauma on children's development and in highlighting the critical need to consider how trauma impacts development (Edwards et al., 2005).

The ACEs study was conducted by the health-maintenance organization Kaiser Permanente and the Centers for Disease Control and Prevention (Felitti et al., 1998). Participants were recruited for the study between 1995 and 1997 and were followed by researchers to assess a variety of outcomes related to health. About half of the participants were female. The average age was 57; 74.8 percent were white; and 75.2 percent had attended college. All participants had jobs and good health care. Participants were asked about ten types of childhood trauma that had been identified by the research on trauma. Five types of trauma were personal: physical abuse, verbal abuse, sexual abuse, physical neglect, and emotional neglect. The remaining five were related to other family members: a parent who was an alcoholic; a mother who was a victim of domestic violence; a family member in jail; a family member diagnosed with a mental illness; and the disappearance of a parent through divorce, death, or abandonment. Researchers then assigned a score to each participant, with each type of trauma counting as one point. For example, a person who had been physically abused, with one alcoholic parent, and a mother who had been beaten would have an ACE score of 3.

The study found that ACEs are extremely common. About two-thirds of individuals reported at least one ACE; 87 percent of individuals who reported one ACE reported at least one additional ACE. Physical and sexual abuse were the most commonly reported ACEs, with 28 percent of study participants reporting physical abuse and 22 percent reporting sexual abuse. Many of the participants reported experiencing a divorce or parental separation or having a parent with a mental and/or substance-use disorder. Another major finding from this study is adverse childhood experiences often occur together. Almost 40 percent of the original sample reported two or more ACEs, and 12.5 percent had experienced four or more.

Researchers have recently examined how ACEs were related to adult outcomes (Felitti, 2009). The number of ACEs a participant reported was strongly associated with high-risk health behaviors such as smoking, alcohol and drug abuse, promiscuity, and severe obesity, as well as poor health including depression, heart disease, cancer, chronic lung disease, and shortened lifespan. Compared to an ACEs score of zero, having four adverse childhood experiences was associated with a seven-fold increase in alcoholism, a doubled risk of being diagnosed with cancer, and a four-fold increase in emphysema. An ACEs score above six was associated with a 460 percent increase in depression and a 1,220 percent increase in attempted suicide. The results from the ACEs study clearly suggest that maltreatment and household dysfunction in childhood contribute to health problems decades later, including chronic diseases—such as heart disease, cancer, stroke, and diabetes—that are the most common causes of death and disability in the United States.

Researchers also examined possible mechanisms that might explain the negative consequences of ACEs on adult health (Felitti, 2009). ACEs can affect the physical body through altering the development of the brain and central nervous system, the immune system, and the endocrine system. Individuals who have experienced adverse events are hyper-alert and in a state of chronic stress. Exposure to prolonged stress disrupts an individual's response to subsequent stressors, which results in hyperarousal and irritability, changes in mood and attachment, challenges to memory, learning difficulties, and increased high-risk and pleasure-seeking behavior. The physical impact of stress and the ACEs also leads to challenges in relationships and behavior.

Additionally, researchers are looking at ways that the ACEs may have effects across generations. The field of epigenetics offers insights into how changes may be passed from one generation to the next and how genes are activated or deactivated by experience or environment. Stress during pregnancy or during interactions between mother and newborn, for example, have been connected to changes in brain structures, immune function, and behaviors later in life. Maternal stress, depression, and exposure to partner violence have all been shown to have epigenetic effects on infants, meaning that the developing fetus's genes are highly susceptible to a mother's distress. The long-term effects of epigenetic dysregulation can be mediated by positive postnatal experiences, if the family is able to provide these supports (Monk, Spicer, and Champagne, 2012).

Research shows that ACEs are common, often occur together, and are related to many risk-taking behaviors and health problems later in life. The more ACEs a child is exposed to, the more likely the child is to experience problems later in life. Clearly, the impact of ACEs has far-reaching consequences, and these findings have led researchers to examine how ACEs affect children.

ACEs Children

The recent *2011/12 National Survey of Children's Health* (http://www.childhealthdata. org/learn/NSCH) provides parent-reported data on nine ACEs reported for children from birth to seventeen years of age in the United States. As shown in the table below, nearly half (47.9 percent) of the children experienced one or more of the nine ACEs measured, and 22.6 percent had experienced two or more. For children from birth to age five, 24 percent had experienced one or more ACEs,

and 12.5 percent had experienced two or more ACEs. The study also found that lower income was connected to higher adverse childhood experiences, highlighting the risks faced by children growing up in poverty.

In a smaller study of children enrolled in a Head Start center, before the children were four years old, 60 percent had an exposure to violence, with a mean ACEs score of more than three, putting these children at a heightened risk for poor developmental outcomes.

Importantly, their parents' mean ACEs score was greater than five, indicating that the parents had experienced high levels of trauma themselves, which may have made it difficult to use more positive parenting techniques with their children. Of the children who had an adverse childhood experience, two-thirds were reported to have a social-emotional concern, based on parents and teacher responses to the Devereux Early Childhood Assessment (DECA), an assessment tool used to measure resilience in young children. Similarly, in a San Francisco pediatric practice, researchers found a relationship between the number of ACEs and reports of learning and behavioral problems in young children. The research on ACEs in children mirrors the adult ACEs studies, showing that adverse experiences in childhood have a great impact on children's ability to thrive and learn. When adults have an opportunity to reflect on their own ACEs, they become more aware of the trauma cycle that they are in with their children. Research with parents who have experienced high ACEs shows that, with proper interventions, they can change their understanding and beliefs about their children's behavior (https://acestoohigh.com/), which in turn can help to open the door of success for both parents and children.

Other Research on Childhood Trauma

In addition to the study of ACEs, researchers in childhood trauma have challenged previous assumptions that infants and young children lack the perception, cognition, and social maturity to remember or understand traumatic events (Zeanah and Zeanah, 2009). Current research confirms that children have the capacity to perceive and remember traumatic events, and researchers have demonstrated that infants and young children have the perceptual ability and memory to be affected by traumatic events. Research has shown, for example, that infants as young as seven months can remember and reenact traumatic events for up to seven years. By eighteen months of age, children begin to develop autobiographical memory comprised of vivid memories including the time and place of events, although verbal recall of events that occurred prior to this time is unlikely.

As researchers investigate the role of childhood trauma on children and adults, organizations such as Zero to Three (https://www.zerotothree.org) and the Center on the Developing Child at Harvard University (http://developingchild.harvard.edu) are sharing critical information with the larger public and aiming to make changes in our society that support what the research is telling us. Both of these organizations provide materials that make the research accessible and can be used in your professional-development efforts and in your work with parents. Information about these two organizations can be found in the Resources section on page 137. Helping early childhood educators and parents understand the importance of risk and protective factors in the lives of children is a great place to start.

The Impact of Early Childhood Trauma on Children's Behavior and Adjustment

Risk and Protective Factors

Recently, there has been a movement to provide trauma-informed practices in many fields, including education, health care, and social work. The push for trauma-informed practices reflects a greater understanding of the scope of trauma in our society. These practices can be used by early childhood educators to deepen their understanding of how trauma is related to challenging behavior and what can be done about it.

Researchers have begun to explore factors that interact, both positively and negatively, with childhood trauma. Parent-child relationships as well as environmental and demographic factors significantly affect outcomes for young children exposed to traumatic events, and these factors may either protect or place a child at greater risk from the adverse effects of trauma.

Young children who are exposed to a traumatic event and also experience a combination of negative sociodemographic factors—such as poverty, minority status, or having a single parent, a teenage parent, or a parent who has not earned a high school diploma or the equivalent—are at greater risk for mental illness (Briggs-Gowan et al., 2010). Additionally, high levels of parental stress are associated with adverse trauma reactions in young children (Crusto et al., 2010), and parental dysfunction, family adversity, residential instability, and problematic parenting can increase the impact of traumatic events (Turner et al., 2012). Young children exposed to chronic and pervasive trauma along with these risk factors are especially vulnerable to experiencing adverse developmental outcomes.

Fortunately, however, there are factors that may help protect young children from the negative impact of trauma. According to trauma expert Bruce D. Perry, safety, stability, and nurturing relationships serve to protect children from the effects of traumatic experience (Perry, 2014). Safety is when a child is free from harm or fear of harm, both physically and socially. Stability indicates consistency in the family environment, and nurturing relationships are when parents, caregivers, and teachers are available and convey a sense of sensitivity and warmth. Nurturing family relationships and relationships with caring, compassionate teachers can insulate children from psychological distress associated with traumatic events. In particular, well-established, secure parent-child relationships are likely to provide protection from negative effects of trauma experienced by young children, and caregiver support and healthy family functioning reduce the risk of psychological distress in young children after a traumatic event. A secure attachment has been shown to help children effectively regulate emotional arousal, and emotional regulation is a critical mechanism that protects young children from extreme trauma reactions.

Relationships and Attachment

Through relationships with important attachment figures, children learn to trust others, regulate their emotions, and interact with the world. They develop a sense of the world as safe or unsafe, and come to understand their own value as individuals. The responsiveness of parents and caregivers to a child's needs is a fundamental building block of secure attachment. A secure attachment is strongly linked to developmental success and helps mitigate traumatic stress. When attachment relationships are unstable or unpredictable, children learn that they cannot rely on others to help them and that the world is not a safe place. When primary caregivers exploit and abuse a child, the child often develops a negative self-concept and feels as if he is a bad person.

Attachment relationships with parents and caregivers build the foundations of social communication. The back and forth of communication between parent and child creates a pattern of "serve and return." (See https://www.youtube.com/watch?v=m_5u8-QSh6A at Harvard's Center on the Developing Child for an excellent video.) The communication between mothers and their infants, organized around face, gaze, and voice, is the basis of early emotional development and physical and emotional coregulation. When they experience a secure attachment with emotionally available parents and caregivers, young children are able to learn and explore.

However, when the parent or caregiver is substantially inconsistent, frightening, neglectful, or abusive, the attachment relationship can be confused and disorganized. Research has linked this type of attachment with later psychopathology. When an infant is neglected, he may be more demanding, anxious, and more difficult to console, developing into a toddler who lacks enthusiasm and is easily frustrated and noncompliant. Keeping our transactional model of relationships in mind, an anxious or crying infant may push an already neglectful parent further away from the child, creating the feedback loop discussed earlier. While abuse and neglect have clear effects on the quality of the attachment relationship, even lesser degrees of impairment in the parent-child relationship can affect attachment. Hence, the importance of a child's close relationship with a caregiver cannot be overestimated.

Effects of Trauma in Young Children

Physical Development and Physical Response

A child continues to develop physically from infancy through adolescence. Biological function and development are greatly influenced by environment—both the physical and the relational. The presence of stress in a child's environment can impair the development of both the brain and nervous system. An absence of mental stimulation in neglectful environments may also limit the brain from developing to its full potential. (See The National Child Traumatic Stress Network website at http://www.nctsn.org.)

When a child grows up afraid or under constant or extreme stress, the immune system and body's stress response systems are altered. Later in life, when the child or adult is exposed to even ordinary levels of stress,

these systems may automatically respond as if the individual is under extreme stress. For example, when an individual faces a stressful situation, he may experience a heightened physiological response such as rapid breathing or heart pounding, or may "freeze" entirely when presented with stressful situations. These individuals may also present with an elevated fight-or-flight or freeze response. In the fight-or-flight response, a child takes an action by trying to defend himself or someone else or by trying to get away. For example, consider a child who, while playing with wooden blocks on the floor, is accidentally bumped by another child. The bumped child immediately becomes enraged, hurling a wooden block toward the other child, who tried to apologize. This child is demonstrating a classic fight response. In a freeze response, a child is either hoping to be left alone or feels powerless and braces herself for pain. In the extreme form of freezing, a child's learned response is dissociation (discussed in a later section).

In addition, children who have experienced complex trauma—defined by the National Child Traumatic Stress Network as children's exposure to multiple traumatic events, often of an invasive, interpersonal nature—frequent-ly suffer from body dysregulation, meaning they may be hyper- or hyporesponsive. For example, they may be hypersensitive to sounds, smells, touch, or light, or they may suffer from anesthesia and analgesia, in which they are unaware of pain, touch, or internal physical sensations. As a result, they may complain of chronic pain in various body areas for which no physical cause can be found, or they may injure themselves without feeling pain or suffer from physical problems without being aware of them.

Emotional Response

When children have experienced early trau-ma, they learn that the world is a dangerous place where loved ones cannot be trusted to protect them. These children are often vigilant and guarded in their interactions with others and are more likely to perceive situations as stressful or dangerous. While this defensive posture is protective when an individual is under attack, it becomes problematic in situations that do not warrant such intense re-actions, such as in the example above when the child attacked another child after being accidentally bumped.

Children who have experienced complex trauma often have difficulty with emotional regulation—identifying, expressing, and man-aging emotions. They often internalize and/or externalize stress reactions, which may result in depression, anxiety, or anger. Their emotional responses may be unpredictable or explosive. For example, a child may seem quiet all morning, even though you know she is having a difficult time at home. Then suddenly, over a minor comment made by another child, she becomes extremely upset.

A child may also react to a reminder of a trau-matic event—a trauma trigger—with trembling, anger, sadness, or avoidance. For a child, reminders of various traumatic events may be everywhere in the environment. Such a child may react often, react powerfully, and have difficulty calming down when upset. Since the traumas are often of an interpersonal nature, even mildly stressful interactions with others may serve as trauma reminders and may trigger intense emotional responses.

Having never learned how to calm them-selves down once they are upset, many of these children become easily overwhelmed. For example, in school they may become so frustrated that they give up on even small tasks that present a challenge, or they may seek to escape a frightening situation by engaging in behavior that results in their being removed from the classroom.

Mental Response

When children grow up under conditions of constant threat, all their internal resources go toward survival. When their bodies and minds have learned to be in chronic-stress response mode, they may have trouble thinking a problem through calmly and considering multiple alternatives. They may find it hard to acquire new skills or take in new information. They may struggle with sustaining attention or curiosity or may be distracted by reactions to trauma reminders. They may show deficits in language development and abstract reasoning skills, resulting in an inability to plan ahead, anticipate the future, and act accordingly. Many children who have experienced complex trauma have learning difficulties that may require support in the academic environment. Children such as these led us to include Essential Feature 4 in the TAGPEC, which asserts that children need access to varying levels of social and emotional support in order to be successful.

Dissociation

When children encounter an overwhelming and terrifying experience, they may *dissociate*, or separate themselves from the experience. One theory is that when confronted with multiple overwhelming and terrifying experiences during their development, children turn on their natural pain system, bracing for an oncoming assault when they are powerless to respond. They may describe their experience by stating that it is as if they are in a dream or some altered state that is not quite real or that it is as if the experience is happening to someone else. Alternately, they may lose all memories or sense of the experiences having happened to them, resulting in gaps in time or even gaps in their personal history. Once they have learned to dissociate as a defense mechanism, they may automatically dissociate during other stressful situations or when faced with reminders of the trauma. Dissociation may affect a child's ability to be fully present in activities, with significant disruptions on a child's sense of time. This in turn may affect learning, classroom behavior, and social interactions. When a child is dissociating, others may not realize it and may think that the child is daydreaming or not paying attention.

Behavior

A child with a complex-trauma history may be easily triggered and is more likely to react very intensely in response to perceived attacks, which may not be attacks at all. The child may struggle with self-regulation and may lack impulse control or the ability to think through consequences before acting. This is why it is difficult for these children to stop and think before acting and why well-meaning teachers can easily get frustrated with children who continue to lack impulse control. In reality, asking these children to stop and think is not getting through to them—they never learned the skill and don't yet have the regulatory capacity to do it. As a result, these children may behave in ways that appear unpredictable, oppositional, volatile, and extreme. A child who feels powerless or who grew up fearing an abusive authority figure may react defensively and aggressively in response to perceived blame or attack, or alternately, may at times be unusually compliant with adults. If a child dissociates often, this will also affect behavior. Such a child may seem detached, distant, or out of touch with reality. Children who experience complex trauma are more likely to engage in high-risk behaviors as they get older, such as self-harm, unsafe sexual practices, and excessive risk taking such as operating a vehicle at high speeds. They may also engage in illegal activities, such as alcohol and substance use, assaulting others, stealing, running away, and/or prostitution, thereby making it more likely that they will enter the juvenile justice system.

Self-Concept and Future Orientation

As reflected in the second assumption of our approach, that relationships guide and regulate behaviors, children learn their self-worth from the reactions of others, particularly those closest to them. Caregivers have the greatest influence on a child's sense of self-worth and value. Abuse and neglect make a child feel worthless and despondent, and a child who is abused will often blame himself for the abuse. The reason for this is that it may feel safer to blame oneself than to recognize the parent as unreliable and dangerous. Shame, guilt, low self-esteem, and a poor self-image are common among children with complex trauma histories. (See The National Child Traumatic Stress Network website at http://www.nctsn.org.)

To plan for the future with a sense of hope and purpose, a child needs to value himself. To plan for the future requires a sense of control and the ability to see one's own actions as having meaning and value. When they are young, children depend on adults to carry this sense of hope for them, to show them a door through which there are meaningful goals and ways to achieve them. In contrast, children who are surrounded by violence in their homes and communities learn from an early age that they cannot trust others, that the world is not safe, and that they are powerless to change their circumstances. Beliefs about themselves, others, and the world diminish their sense of competency. Their negative expectations interfere with their ability to problem solve in productive and positive ways, and these expectations shut down opportunities for them to believe they have to power or agency to make a difference in their own lives. A child with a complex trauma history may view himself as powerless, "damaged," and/or may perceive the world as a meaningless place in which planning and positive action are futile. Quite simply, these children have trouble feeling hopeful. Having learned to operate in survival mode, the child lives from moment to moment without pausing to think about, plan for, or even dream about a future.

Symptoms of Trauma in Early Childhood

A child's response to traumatic experiences can show up in many different ways and will vary from child to child. Often, children reexperience trauma and will act out a trauma in an attempt to resolve it. For example, a child may continuously reenact themes from a traumatic event through play. A child who has seen his father act abusively toward his mother, for example, may pretend to make a boy doll attack and hit a girl doll. Triggers may remind children of the traumatic event and a preoccupation may develop (Lieberman and Knorr, 2007). Nightmares, flashbacks, and dissociative episodes also are symptoms of trauma in young children (De Young et al., 2011).

Some young children exposed to traumatic experiences may avoid conversations, people, objects, places, or situations that remind them of the trauma (Coates and

Gaensbauer, 2009). They also frequently have diminished interest in play or other activities and withdraw from relationships. Hyperarousal such as temper tantrums, increased irritability, disturbed sleep, a constant state of alertness, difficulty concentrating, exaggerated startle responses, increased physical aggression, and increased activity levels are also common symptoms. (De Young et al., 2011).

After experiencing trauma, young children may exhibit changes in eating and sleeping patterns, become easily frustrated, experience increased separation anxiety, develop enuresis (bedwetting) or encopresis (loss of bowel control), or lose acquired developmental skills (Zindler, Hogan, and Graham, 2010). Children with complex trauma histories may develop chronic or recurrent physical complaints, such as headaches or stomachaches. If sexual trauma is experienced, a child may exhibit sexualized behaviors inappropriate for his age

(Goodman, Miller, and West-Olatunji, 2012; Zero to Three, 2005).

The symptoms that young children experience as a result of exposure to a traumatic experience overlap with other childhood issues. Many of the symptoms of trauma exposure look like early mental-health conditions such as depression, separation anxiety, attention-deficit/hyperactivity disorder (ADHD), oppositional defiant disorder (ODD), or other developmental crises (American Psychiatric Association, 2013). It is important to resist giving young children diagnoses based on symptoms only. A good clinician will take time to get a complete history and will seek input on how the child behaves in different settings. The early childhood setting can provide vital information about the child's behavior. Because young children have such varied responses to trauma experiences, it is critical to always consider trauma and other stressors when assessing a child's behavior.

What to Look For

Because young children do not always have the words to tell us what has happened to them or how they feel, we need to look for symptoms and behaviors to help us understand a child's world. Children who have ongoing or previous trauma experience may show similar symptoms and behaviors. Often, sudden changes in behavior can be a sign of trauma exposure.

As a pediatrician and a clinician, when we take a comprehensive history, we look for developmental change, such as when a child loses or regresses in a previous mastered stage of development. Often, we see toileting accidents in a child who was previously potty-trained or we may see the use of baby talk in a child who previously communicated at age level. We may

also see children who no longer are making developmental progress as expected.

Another symptom that we as clinicians look for is change in a child's biology and physiology, such as difficulty with sleep at nap time or bedtime. This may include avoiding sleep, waking up from sleep, or nightmares. Changes in the child's appetite and/or toileting routine are also common. After a traumatic event, children may over- or underreact to physical contact, bright lighting, sudden movements, or loud sounds

> Because young children have such varied responses to trauma experiences, it is critical to always consider trauma and other stressors when assessing a child's behavior.

such as slamming doors or sirens. As children become older, they may have increased somatic complaints such as headaches, stomachaches, or overreaction to minor bumps and bruises. Parents, caregivers, and teachers may notice increased distress such as a child being unusually whiny, irritable, or moody.

We also ask about changes in behaviors and relationships. Children may develop new, unspecific fears such as a fear of the dark or monsters or specific fears about their own safety or the safety of others. We often see an increase in angry outbursts, a decrease in attention and focus, and/or withdrawal from activities or other children.

What You Can Do

Trauma can undermine children's ability to learn, form relationships, and function appropriately in the early childhood setting. It can disrupt the development of language and communication skills; the ability to understand cause-and-effect relationships; the ability to take another person's perspective; attentiveness to classroom tasks and executive functions, such as goal setting, planning, and anticipating consequences; and the ability to engage in structured environments. Becoming aware of the scope of and the signs and symptoms of childhood trauma is the first step to developing a plan to help a traumatized child.

Because a child who has experienced trauma feels a loss of safety and may feel powerless, you should maintain usual routines and ensure that they are consistent and predictable. Routines create a sense of normalcy and communicate the message that the child is safe and the environment is stable. In addition, providing a child with choices helps her regain a sense of control.

Alternatively, we may see increased separation anxiety or clinginess toward teachers or other primary caregivers. Another change is that a child may start asking questions about death and dying.

It's important to note that not all of these symptoms are indicative of trauma. Some of these changes, such as an increase in clinginess, may be developmental; for example, when a child is around eight months old, he may begin to experience separation anxiety. Certain changes such as re-creating the traumatic event through repeatedly talking about, playing out, or drawing the event and worry about recurrence of the traumatic event are more clearly indicative of trauma exposure.

For a child who has experienced trauma, it is also important to set clear, firm limits for inappropriate behavior and to develop logical consequences. Punitive consequences, which are inconsistent with the humanistic approach to behavior guidance, can lead to escalation of the behavior and the potential for retraumatizing the child. Since behavior is bidirectional in nature, it is particularly important for caregivers and teachers to respond to behaviors without their own escalation. For example, if warnings become louder, a child may experience a trauma trigger. When caregivers can remain emotionally regulated, they are available to coregulate the child.

Early childhood educators can help children by being sensitive to the cues in the environment that may cause a reaction in the traumatized child. For example, victims of natural disasters such as an earthquake might react badly to the ground moving under their feet when the class takes a field trip to the beach. A child who has been sexually abused may pull away angrily when a teacher tries to reach out to comfort him. You can anticipate such difficult times and provide additional support. It is important to recognize that many situations may be triggers for children who have experienced trauma. If you are able to identify triggers, you can help by preparing the child for the situation by warning children if you will be doing something out of the ordinary, such as turning off the lights or making a sudden loud noise. Children may increase problem behaviors near an anniversary of a traumatic event, and being aware of and planning for this allows you to provide extra support when a child needs it the most.

A child who has experienced trauma may require more support and encouragement than a typical child. It is critical to help the child know which teacher is there to help and is available to provide additional support if needed. You can make sure to provide a safe place for the child to talk about what happened and let the child know that is okay to talk about what happened. When a child asks questions about traumatic events, give him simple, clear, and realistic answers and clarify distortions and misconceptions. You may want to practice the conversation with another adult before you talk with the child. Early childhood educators need to understand that children cope by reenacting trauma through play or through their interactions with others. Resist their efforts to draw you into a negative repetition of the trauma.

Another critical area of the early childhood setting for a child who has experienced trauma is peer interactions. A child's hypervigilance and inability to regulate emotional states after maltreatment often results in challenging behaviors during peer interactions. Converse-ly, other children's reactions to the trauma-tized child need to be monitored as well. It is important to listen to the information they share with you and to protect the traumatized child from peers' curiosity, while at the same time protecting classmates from the details of a child's trauma.

Working with traumatized children can be daunting. It is important to know you are not alone but part of a team caring for a child. As a leader in the field of early education, you can take the initiative to ensure that your staff is trained in trauma-informed care, including knowledge of the symptoms of trauma in children. You can introduce strategies that are known to help teachers reflect on their own perceptions of behavior so that they can be more intentional and nonreactive when working with children with complex trauma histories. Such strategies might include reflective supervision, logging and journaling, and team discussions.

If you have identified a child who has experienced trauma, it is important to reach out to your teachers to ensure that they know how to use the strategies known to help trauma-tized children. Teachers may need time to engage in trauma-related professional development and technical assistance. We suggest becoming trauma informed, so that you can be a guide for others. The National Child Traumatic Stress Network has developed an informative toolkit for educators, which we believe is a good place to start (https://wmich.edu/sites/default/files/attachments/u57/2013/child-trauma-toolkit.pdf).

Another key action that leaders can take to effectively help students who have experienced trauma is to inform your program's administration and mental-health professional of your concerns. If your program doesn't have a higher administration or mental-health professional, then we encourage you to reach outside your program to access community referrals, where you can get more information and support and where you can learn how to support the child. We talk more about these types of referrals in the next section, and a list of resources is provided in the Resources section on page 137.

The Role of the Adult and the Importance of Relationships

Children's early experiences have a profound effect on their later development—physically, emotionally, cognitively, and socially. The relationships young children have with parents, caregivers, relatives, teachers, and peers are critical to their ability to learn about and navigate the world around them. These key relationships shape the architecture of the developing brain and influence a child's lifelong mental health. Disruptions in a child's process of development can impair her ability to learn and relate to others, with lifelong implications. At a societal level, many costly problems, from school failure to chronic health issues to homelessness, could be dramatically reduced by improving children's relationships and experiences early in life.

The critical role of responsive adults in promoting young children's social-emotional development is consistent with the first and second assumptions of the humanistic approach to behavior guidance presented in chapter 1: **The role of the adult is to teach children appropriate social-emotional skills. Relationships guide and regulate behaviors.**

Unfortunately, many young children are frequently exposed to traumatic events and are particularly vulnerable to these events when they do occur. Because early childhood is a period of rapid growth and development, trauma can negatively affect children during critical periods of development. Young children are dependent upon caregivers, and they lack the coping skills needed to deal with adversity. They are highly impressionable; therefore, traumatic events can deeply affect a child's sense of safety. The good news is that a skillful, attuned parent, caregiver, or teacher can help mitigate the effects of traumatic events. Helping parents, caregivers, and teachers understand the impact of trauma on child development and teaching them the skills needed to help children process their emotions can greatly benefit young children who have been exposed to trauma.

In our work as a pediatrician and as a child psychiatrist, we often first meet children when they are at risk of being kicked out of preschool. Quite frequently, these children come to us with well-meaning, nonclinical diagnoses such as ADHD or ODD. Sometimes they are labeled as being "just a bad kid." Luckily, over the last five years in our community, we are beginning to shift the perspective from "What is wrong with this child?" to "What is happening in this child's life?" and "What happened in this child's development that is affecting him now?" This shift in questions leads to much greater compassion for a child who may be suffer-

> The good news is that a skillful, attuned parent, caregiver, or teacher can help mitigate the effects of traumatic events.

ing silently. Now, when a child misbehaves, many of our early childhood colleagues are considering the role of childhood trauma and stress. The focus on behavior as the

problem, rather than viewing the child as the problem, is consistent with the third assumption of the humanistic approach to behavior guidance: **Behavior is communication.**

Behavior Is Communication

As discussed in chapter 2, a child's behavior reflects her biology, relationships, and environment. The connection between a child's development and her relationships, particularly the primary attachment relationship, has been studied for many years. Children's relationships throughout their development influence their biology, which in turn greatly influences their relationships and their ability to develop future relationships. For example, when babies reach out to caregivers through babbling, facial expressions, and gestures and adults respond with similar vocalizations, expressions, and gestures, then the baby's brain architecture is strengthened. The baby is likely to reach out to adults again when her actions toward the world are met with warmth and consistency. In this way, relationships and biology are interconnected in a feedback loop that involves a dynamic process of growth, stress, and regulation. When viewed this way, it becomes clear that each child's behavior is far from simple; rather, behavior has emerged from the complex interplay of the child's biology and environment.

Additionally, and as described in chapter 2, the various environments in which a child is embedded influence both the child and caregivers. We refer to the bidirectional, interdependent effects of the child and environment as transactional in nature (Sameroff and MacKenzie, 2003). For example, if a child shows negative behaviors and the parent responds harshly and/or inconsistently, then the interactions tend to grow more negative over time (Stepp et al., 2012). Therefore, when we observe a child's behavior, we can wonder about her past experiences, relationships, and environments, as this enables us to help provide safe, stable, and nurturing relationships and environments in the present to hopefully help that child to have a brighter future.

It is important to note that each child handles experiences differently, reflecting the fourth assumption of the humanistic approach to behavior guidance: **Each child is a unique individual.**

Each Child Is a Unique Individual

Some traumatic experiences are single events, such as a dog bite, while others are ongoing and repeated, such as sexual abuse. Fundamentally, these traumatic experiences can leave children with an overwhelming sense of fear and loss, making them feel unsafe and as if they have no control over their lives. Traumatic experiences are so powerful and dangerous that they overwhelm a child's capacity to regulate her emotions.

For some children, these feelings become so intense that they get in the way of the child's continued physical, emotional, social, and/or cognitive development. Unaddressed, trauma can have long-term effects on the quality and length of a person's life.

The subjective experience of the child determines the impact of traumatic event. Whereas one child may react extremely to a traumatic situation, another child may be less affected by the same situation. Developmental and cultural factors also play a role in trauma responses. Learning how to understand, process, and cope with difficulties, even trauma, is a natural part of a child's developmental process. Without help, it is easy for a child to get stuck and unable to process an overwhelming experience. A single event, such as a dog bite, without resolution, for example, can lead to problems similar to more complex trauma. Some children who receive support will recover within a few weeks or months from the fear and anxiety caused by a traumatic experience. Other children, however, will need more help over a longer period of time to heal and may need continuing support from family, teachers, or mental-health professionals. Symptoms, feelings, and behaviors may recur during anniversaries of the event or when children see media reports that may act as reminders of the trauma.

Some children show signs of stress in the first few weeks after a trauma but quickly return to their usual state of physical and emotional health. Even when children do not exhibit serious symptoms initially, they may experience some degree of emotional distress, which may continue or even deepen over a long period of time. Many children who have experienced traumatic events

may experience problems that impair their day-to-day functioning. These children may have behavioral problems; however, there are many other children whose suffering may not be apparent at all. It is important to be aware of both the children who act out and the quiet children who do not appear to have behavioral problems. These quiet children often never get the help they need, despite being in just as much pain as the child who throws a chair across the room or hits other children.

The multiple ways that trauma-related anxiety can show up in children can lead to misdiagnosis. Many post-traumatic stress behaviors seen in children are nearly identical to those of children with developmental delays, ADHD, and other mental-health conditions. Without recognition of the possibility that a child is experiencing childhood traumatic stress, we may develop a plan that does not fully address the child's needs with regard to trauma. Because childhood trauma is so common and presents in so many different ways, it is important to educate parents and early childhood providers about the effects of trauma. We believe that education about trauma and behavioral responses will help teachers respond more accurately and fairly to children's behavior, reflecting the fifth assumption of the humanistic approach to behavior guidance: **Implicit bias affects decision making.**

Implicit Bias Affects Decision Making

Earlier in this book, we described how a teacher's implicit or unconscious biases affect how he interprets and responds to challenging behaviors. For example, when confronted with a situation in which a child is behaving aggressively toward others, teachers (like many people) often respond automatically, relying on their previous ex-

periences and beliefs as a guide. While this can be an efficient way to at least temporarily stop the behavior, it can lead the teacher to make decisions that are based on unconscious, unexamined beliefs, some of which may reflect stereotypes about the child rather than truths. Acting on unconscious beliefs, as Gilliam's (2016) study has shown, can lead to inequities in the classroom, including suspending and expelling particular children more than others for the same behavior.

Children who have experienced trauma are at an increased risk of experiencing the negative effects of teachers' implicit biases. As we discussed earlier in this chapter, trauma affects children's behavior in a range of complex ways that can be easily misunderstood by teachers as disrespect (avoidance), aggression (anger), and/or defiance (depression). It is therefore critical for early childhood teachers to have opportunities to engage in reflective activities that bring implicit biases to the forefront of awareness and challenge the truthfulness of these biases in the face of what we know about childhood trauma.

Accessing Trauma-Informed Mental-Health Providers and Community Resources

Trauma-informed mental-health professionals are effective in helping children deal with traumatic stress reactions. There is a growing body of evidence-based therapies that is being tracked by the National Traumatic Stress Network. Mental-health professionals trained in trauma can help caregivers and teachers reestablish a safe environment and a sense of safety as children return to normal routines. A key component of what mental-health-care professionals do is to meet with children in a safe, accepting environment where there is an opportunity to talk about and make sense of the traumatic experience. Trained clinicians can support the child in verbalizing feelings rather than engaging in inappropriate behavior. They are trained to explain the trauma and answer questions in a simple and age-appropriate manner. Trauma-informed mental health professionals can also teach children, caregivers, and teachers techniques for dealing with overwhelming emotional reactions. They involve primary caregivers in the healing process and connect caregivers to resources to address their needs because young children's level of distress often mirrors their caregiver's level of distress. It is essential to treat young children's mental-health problems within the context of their families, homes, and communities.

Secondary Trauma

Working with traumatized children and their families affects those who care for them. Caregivers and teachers are at high risk for burnout and secondary trauma. Burnout is a state of emotional, mental, and physical exhaustion caused by excessive and prolonged stress. It occurs when you feel overwhelmed, emotionally drained, and unable to meet constant demands. As the stress continues, you begin to lose the interest or motivation that led you to take on a certain role in the first place. Secondary traumatic stress is the emotional duress that results when an individual hears about the trauma experiences of another person. It has similar symptoms to post-traumatic stress disorder (PTSD). Individuals affected by secondary stress may notice an increase in arousal and avoidance reactions related to the indirect trauma exposure. They may experience changes in memory and perception; alterations in their sense of self-efficacy; a depletion of personal resources; and disruption in their perceptions of safety, trust, and independence. Because trauma is common, individuals and organizations need to have policy and resources to protect staff who are interacting with trauma-exposed children and their families. We encourage administrators to consider ways to build in the topic of secondary trauma in their professional-development efforts with teachers.

Advocacy for Trauma Supports in Early Childhood Education

The early childhood community is an integral part of young children's lives and is an important partner with other professionals who care for young children. Providers of early care and education must be better equipped to understand and manage the emotional and behavioral problems of young children exposed to trauma. It is for this reason that we advocate for more trauma-focused professional training and easier access to child-mental-health professionals when they are needed. We as a community of providers who help young children and their families need to work together to increase resources for our children and for the individuals who care for them.

The principles of trauma-informed care hold great potential for helping people to recover from the effects of adverse childhood experiences. According to a concept paper published in 2014 by the Substance Abuse and Mental Health Services Administration (SAMHSA), a program, organization, or system that is trauma informed realizes the widespread impact of trauma and understands potential paths for recovery; recognizes the signs and symptoms of trauma in clients, families, staff, and others involved with the system; re-sponds by fully integrating knowledge about trauma into policies, procedures, practices; and seeks to actively resist retraumatization (Center for Behavioral Health Statistics and Quality, 2015).

The application of trauma-informed care can help to create supportive environments with positive relationships that empower trauma survivors to explore alternative choices and go through more hopeful and productive doors to the future. There are numerous resources available to help leaders become familiar with the principles and actions related to trauma-informed care, many of which are listed in the Resources section on page 137. As a starting point, we recommend exploring information on the National Center for Trauma Informed Care website (https://www.nasmhpd.org/content/national-center-trauma-informed-care-nctic-0). The more that we, as early childhood leaders and professionals, learn to support all children in the development of healthy coping strategies, the more likely it is that these children are going to grow up resilient. In line with our humanistic approach to behavior guidance, we believe that we can work to help children and families learn, grow, and live to their fullest potential.

Some Concluding Thoughts

At the beginning of this book, we encouraged you to envision what the door to the future looks like for the children, families, and staff in your early childhood program. Our hope is that reading this book and using the TAGPEC to revise or create a behavior-guidance policy for your program has helped to reframe your understanding of discipline. We hope that you will include a humanistic approach reflecting the belief that all children have the inherent ability to reach their individual potential—to be their very best self. And finally, we hope that we have provided you with the tools you need to help children open the door to a future that is filled with unlimited possibilities for success.

Appendices

Appendix A: The Teaching and Guidance Policy Essentials Checklist ✔ TAGPEC

Program's name: _____

Date filled out: _____

Completed by: _____

Role in program: _____

Instructions: This checklist is designed to identify different aspects of quality in early care and education guidance policies. This checklist can be completed by a trained program staff member or a specialist in early care and education.

For each question below, please check the response that best describes your program's guidance policy. Check *no* if the policy does not show evidence of addressing the item. Check *emerging* if your policy shows some evidence of addressing the item. Check *yes* if the policy shows clear evidence of addressing the item.

Essential Feature 1: Intentional Focus on Teaching Social-Emotional Skills

Early childhood behavior-guidance policies should reflect an instructional, proactive approach to behavior guidance that supports the learning and practice of appropriate prosocial behavior of all children, regardless of individual differences and/or cultural and linguistic background.

Item 1: The policy clearly states that the goal of behavior guidance is to teach social-emotional skills to all children.

☐ Yes   ☐ Emerging   ☐ No

Item 2: The policy clearly describes the role of the teacher in proactively teaching all children social-emotional skills.

☐ Yes   ☐ Emerging   ☐ No

Item 3: The policy clearly describes the role of positive and consistent interactions among teachers and children in promoting positive behavior.

☐ Yes   ☐ Emerging   ☐ No

Item 4: Multiple, evidence-based, developmentally and culturally appropriate strategies are described.

☐ Yes   ☐ Emerging   ☐ No

Essential Feature 2: Developmentally and Culturally Appropriate Learning Environment

Early childhood behavior-guidance policies should describe the importance of a developmentally appropriate learning environment that is predictable, engaging, and relationship based.

Item 5: The policy clearly describes the importance of nurturing and responsive teacher-child relationships as essential to preventing challenging behaviors.

☐ Yes   ☐ Emerging   ☐ No

Item 6: The policy emphasizes the importance of the sufficient and active adult supervision of all children.

☐ Yes   ☐ Emerging   ☐ No

Item 7: The policy describes the need for staff to continuously (at all times) monitor and respond to children's behavior.

☐ Yes   ☐ Emerging   ☐ No

Item 8: The policy clearly describes the use of ecological arrangements, such as classroom environment and materials, as a means for promoting positive, prosocial behavior.

☐ Yes   ☐ Emerging   ☐ No

Item 9: The policy clearly describes the need for a predictable, intentional, and developmentally appropriate daily schedule, including for example small and large group times, carefully planned transitions, and child- and adult-initiated activities.

☐ Yes   ☐ Emerging   ☐ No

Item 10: The policy clearly describes the value of an engaging curriculum that takes a strengths-based view of culture and language as a deterrent to challenging behavior.

☐ Yes   ☐ Emerging   ☐ No

Essential Feature 3: Setting Behavioral Expectations

Early childhood behavior-guidance policies should describe clear and consistent expectations for behavior.

Item 11: The policy has clearly stated program-wide behavioral expectations that are developmentally appropriate and reflect the natural learning abilities typically associated with the age groups of children served. If this item is answered *no*, then items 12–15 must be answered *no*.

☐ Yes   ☐ Emerging   ☐ No

Item 12: Behavioral expectations are stated positively and emphasize what children can and should do rather than what they cannot do.

☐ Yes   ☐ Emerging   ☐ No

Item 13: Behavioral expectations are designed to promote children's self-regulation, promoting external to internal foci from staff to self.

☐ Yes   ☐ Emerging   ☐ No

Item 14: The policy describes the need for clearly defined rules that are observable and measurable at the classroom level.

☐ Yes   ☐ Emerging   ☐ No

Item 15: The policy describes the need for a connection between program-level behavioral expectations and classroom rules.

☐ Yes   ☐ Emerging   ☐ No

Item 16: The policy clearly describes practices that are unacceptable for use by staff, such as humiliation or depriving meals, snacks, rest, and so on.

☐ Yes   ☐ Emerging   ☐ No

Essential Feature 4: Preventing and Addressing Challenging Behaviors Using a Tiered Model of Intervention

Early childhood behavior-guidance policies should identify primary, secondary, and tertiary preventative and intervention practices for promoting prosocial behavior and reducing challenging behavior in young children.

Item 17: Procedures are in place to screen children for behavioral concerns.

☐ Yes   ☐ Emerging   ☐ No

Item 18: The policy clearly describes the need to understand challenging behavior as children's effort to communicate.

☐ Yes   ☐ Emerging   ☐ No

Item 19: The policy clearly describes primary strategies to teach and reinforce prosocial behaviors in all children. (See Items 1–10).

☐ Yes   ☐ Emerging   ☐ No

Item 20: The policy describes targeted secondary strategies, such as the use of social-skills curricula and intentional small-group instruction, for children who are at risk for problem behaviors.

☐ Yes   ☐ Emerging   ☐ No

Item 21: The policy clearly describes the use of tertiary strategies, such as developing a behavior-support plan, early childhood mental health consultation, and trauma-informed care, for helping children who exhibit chronic and intense problem behaviors.

☐ Yes   ☐ Emerging   ☐ No

Essential Feature 5: Working with Families

Early childhood behavior-guidance policies should reflect the family-centered nature of early childhood education.

Item 22: The policy promotes proactive rather than reactive collaborative relationships as a means of promoting social competence in children.

☐ Yes   ☐ Emerging   ☐ No

Item 23: The policy promotes authentic staff-family collaboration in effectively dealing with challenging behavior, and families are given an opportunity to participate in developing and implementing interventions.

☐ Yes   ☐ Emerging   ☐ No

Item 24: The policy describes the need for obtaining contextually and culturally relevant information, such as at-home sleeping and eating habits, family events, and favorite toys and activities, from families in order to understand children's inappropriate behavior.

☐ Yes   ☐ Emerging   ☐ No

Item 25: The policy promotes embedding individual behavior-support-plan goals and objectives into family-home routines and activities.

☐ Yes   ☐ Emerging   ☐ No

Essential Feature 6: Staff Training and Professional Development

Early childhood behavior-guidance policies should ensure that staff have access to training and technical assistance in implementing policy guidelines and promoting the social competence of young children.

Item 26: The policy describes practices that are in place to ensure that staff understand and can articulate the behavior-guidance policy.

☐ Yes   ☐ Emerging   ☐ No

Item 27: The policy describes a process for ongoing professional-development opportunities to support staff in the use of evidence-based prevention and intervention strategies.

☐ Yes   ☐ Emerging   ☐ No

Item 28: The policy describes the intent of the program to ensure that staff have a strong understanding of culture and diversity and are provided opportunities to engage in self-reflection and ongoing professional development that encourage awareness of implicit and explicit biases that may affect their work with children and families.

☐ Yes   ☐ Emerging   ☐ No

Essential Feature 7: Use of Data for Continuous Improvement

Early childhood behavior-guidance policies should reference the use of a data-collection system by which the relative success or failure of the behavior-guidance policy will be evaluated.

Item 29: Policy-evaluation procedures are in place and clearly describe how the success or failure of the policy will be measured.

☐ Yes   ☐ Emerging   ☐ No

Item 30: The policy describes how data will be used to engage in continuous improvement to ensure that practices are in line with the intent of the behavior-guidance policy and to ensure fairness and equity for all children.

☐ Yes   ☐ Emerging   ☐ No

Do you have any concerns about your program's guidance policy?

☐ No   ☐ Some   ☐ Yes

If you responded *some* or *yes*, please describe your concerns below.

_____

_____

_____

_____

Scoring the TAGPEC

Steps

Step 1: Calculate score total. *No* = 0   *Emerging* = 1   *Yes* = 2

Step 2: Sum all of the item scores to get a total score.

Step 3: Enter the essential feature scores on the summary section.

Step 4: Enter the total score on the summary section.

Step 5: Higher item scores are strengths.

Summary Section

Essential Feature	Subscale Total Score	Number of Items	Average Score
EF 1: Intentional Teaching Approach Item 1: _____ Item 2: _____ Item 3: _____ Item 4: _____		$\div\ 4$	$=$
EF 2: Developmentally Appropriate Learning Environment Item 5: _____ Item 6: _____ Item 7: _____ Item 8: _____ Item 9: _____ Item 10: _____		$\div\ 6$	$=$
EF 3: Setting Behavioral Expectations Item 11: _____ Item 12: _____ Item 13: _____ Item 14: _____ Item 15: _____ Item 16: _____		$\div\ 6$	$=$
EF 4: Tiered Model of Intervention Item 17: _____ Item 18: _____ Item 19: _____ Item 20: _____ Item 21: _____		$\div\ 5$	$=$
EF 5: Working with Families Item 22: _____ Item 23: _____ Item 24: _____ Item 25: _____		$\div\ 4$	$=$
EF 6: Staff Training and Professional Development Item 26: _____ Item 27: _____ Item 28: _____		$\div\ 3$	$=$
EF 7: Data Monitoring and Improvement Item 29: _____ Item 30: _____		$\div\ 2$	$=$
Total: _____		$\div\ 30$	$=$

Comments Section

Policy Strengths:

_____

_____

_____

_____

_____

_____

_____

_____

Policy Areas for Improvement:

_____

_____

_____

_____

_____

_____

_____

_____

_____

_____

Appendix B: Strategies to Reduce Implicit Bias in Early Childhood Settings

The strategies listed on this page come from the Kirwan Institute for the Study of Race and Ethnicity at The Ohio State University. We have selected these strategies for inclusion in our book because they are based on research, reflect our humanistic approach to behavior guidance and our commitment to equity, acknowledge the importance of the early childhood years as critical to prevention and early intervention, and reflect how implicit bias can be addressed at both organizational and individual levels.

School-Wide and Organizational Strategies: Considering Institutional Values

Decision-Making Practices: Institutional values that may help prevent bias during critical decision points		TAGPEC Essential Feature
Data-Based Decision Making	• Use of data collection, monitoring, and accountability when developing and implementing educational and discipline policies • Use of data to shed light on trends and patterns that may otherwise go unnoticed by individuals involved in decision making	**EF 7: Use of Data for Continuous Improvement** Early childhood behavior-guidance policies should reference the use of a data-collection system by which the relative success or failure of the behavior-guidance policy will be evaluated.
Culturally Representative Schools	• Consideration given to how images of students and staff support the commitment to equity • Consideration of what images communicate or suggest about who is successful, included, or excluded • Images do not confirm stereotyped associations • Mindful of how values are communicated through images and other forms of messaging • High expectations for disabled and minority youth in all domains	**EF 1: Intentional Focus on Teaching Social-Emotional Skills** Early childhood behavior-guidance policies should reflect an instructional, proactive approach to behavior guidance that supports the learning and practice of appropriate prosocial behavior of all children, regardless of individual differences and/or cultural and linguistic background. **EF 2: Developmentally Appropriate Learning Environment** Early childhood behavior-guidance policies should describe the importance of a developmentally and culturally appropriate learning environment that is predictable, engaging, and relationship based.

Decision-Making Practices: Institutional values that may help prevent bias during critical decision points		TAGPEC Essential Feature
Staff Culture/ Development	• Use professional-development time to provide opportunities for education on implicit bias and other types of cultural-competency–focused training • Create an atmosphere where staff can identify, discuss, and find solutions for instances of bias	**EF 6: Staff Training and Professional Development** The policy describes practices that are in place to ensure that staff understand and can articulate the behavior-guidance policy. (Item 28 refers specifically to implicit bias.)

Student-Level Strategies

| **Classroom Instruction** | • Use materials and photos that counter stereotypical associations

• Ensure that all races are represented in positions of power | **EF1: Intentional Focus on Teaching Social-Emotional Skills**

Early childhood behavior-guidance policies should reflect an instructional, proactive approach to behavior guidance that supports the learning and practice of appropriate prosocial behavior of all children, regardless of individual differences and/or cultural and linguistic background.

EF 2: Developmentally Appropriate Learning Environment

Early childhood behavior-guidance policies should describe the importance of a developmentally and culturally appropriate learning environment that is predictable, engaging, and relationship based. |

Effective Discipline Policies: How to Create a System that Supports Young Children's Social-Emotional Competence

| Classroom Dynamics | • Facilitate intergroup contact between peers

• Utilize interventions focused on stress reduction | **EF 4: Preventing and Addressing Challenging Behaviors Using a Tiered Model of Intervention**

Early childhood behavior-guidance policies should identify primary, secondary, and tertiary preventative and intervention practices for promoting prosocial behavior and reducing challenging behavior in young children. |
| Decrease Ambiguity in Behavior Management and Discipline | • Provide examples of behavior expectations in measurable terms

• Ensure behavior expectations are highly visible throughout the school | **EF 3: Setting Behavioral Expectations**

Early childhood behavior-guidance policies should describe clear and consistent expectations for behavior. |

Appendix C: Sample High-Quality Behavior-Guidance Policies

Imagination Children's Center Behavior Support Plan

Mission

It is the goal of all staff at Imagination Children's Center that children learn to guide their own behavior and to internalize self-discipline. We believe that the social-emotional learning during the early years sets the tone for a child's ongoing experiences in educational settings. The role of the teacher is, therefore, to guide children toward learning how to solve their own problems and to provide them with the tools to do so.

We believe that young children deserve careful attention to every aspect of their social-emotional development. They are complex individuals worthy of respect and the recognition that they are each unique, valuable, capable, and lovable. Each child comes to our program with a unique set of defining characteristics, including family background, abilities, temperament, and learning styles. Positive relationships between children and adults are fundamental to a harmonious environment that promotes optimal growth.

Master teachers will read the developmental histories of all of the children in the classroom. Updates will be made at least annually to continue to capture new information; for example, does the family have any developmental or behavioral concerns regarding the child? How does the child typically behave at home and outside the home?

Families as Partners

We believe that parents are the primary educators of the child. The home is the child's first and continual learning environment. Children come to school with different life experiences and skills that we acknowledge and draw upon as we plan for and facilitate new learning. Parents have an in-depth knowledge of their children. When parents share this knowledge, teachers can better understand each child.

We believe that parents are our partners. We recognize that a child's home is the first and most important place of learning. Any information you give us concerning your family's culture, rituals, or challenges helps us better understand your child's needs. By becoming involved with the classroom, you are supporting our philosophy of partnership and making a link between home and school. We invite your involvement in the classroom; you may, for example, help out with a special activity, an ongoing activity, and/or field trips.

We believe that communication with parents on all levels is important. Families receive program- and classroom-specific newsletters at least quarterly. Upcoming events and activities are posted by the front door and on each classroom's bulletin board. Teachers make an effort to talk with each child's parent at least once a day. The classrooms also have a notebook where parents can leave notes in writing. Check your child's cubby daily for work to go home and for information that is posted for you.

Parent conferences are an important way that we get to know you and your child. Upon enrollment, your child's classroom teacher will schedule a "Getting to Know You" conference. This conference is designed to find out about your child, family, routines, traditions, and at-home strategies. In this way we can aid in your child's transition to school and support his or her learning style. In January, we have a "Winter Check In." This is a time when we check in with families and let you know briefly how your child is doing at school. In the spring we prepare for a more in-depth conference. This is a chance for the teachers to share information they have gathered about your child's development using our assessment tool, the High/Scope Child Observation Record COR and the Ages and Stages Questionnaires (ASQ). You are welcome and encouraged to ask for a conference with teachers or our directors at any time during the year.

Program-Wide Developmentally Appropriate Behavior Expectations

Our staff will use a positive guidance approach, which enables a child to develop self-control and assume responsibility for his or her own behavior. We will foster and guide a child's choices so his or her behavior will reflect peaceful human relationships with other children and adults. We emphasize the importance of establishing and fostering positive relationships between adults and children. We will provide an age-appropriate, engaging, and culturally appropriate learning environment and a curriculum that is stimulating and conducive to the development of a positive self-image in each child.

Each class at Imagination Children's Center uses the same basic rules, which are as follows:

1   We keep ourselves safe. (We listen to the teacher; we stay with the group.)

2   We keep each other safe. (We use safe touches; we listen to one another.)

3   We keep our things safe.

Evidenced-Based and Developmentally Appropriate Behavior-Guidance Techniques

The following techniques are developmentally appropriate and best practice, and all employees are expected to know and use these behavior-guidance techniques.

- Tell children what you want them to do, instead of telling them what not to do.

- Active listening: Interpreting feelings and reflecting them back to the child. This encourages acceptance and trust.

- Redirection: Moving the child's attention to a more appropriate activity, when he or she is behaving inappropriately. Usually the behavior that is being avoided isn't even discussed.

- Modifying the environment: Childproofing, simplifying, limiting, or enriching the environment as needed.

- Reinforcing and noticing: Helping children feel important, acknowledged, and validated.

- Setting limits: Helping children understand the need to respect the rights of others; to ensure safety of the child and others; and to respect people, materials, animals, and the environment.

- Enforcing natural consequences: Consequences should be an outgrowth of the child's behavior. They serve as a way to teach tangible cause and effect as it applies to behavior, and they help children learn responsibility for the behavior.

- Negotiation: The teacher identifies the problem, encourages the children to contribute ideas to solve the problem, helps facilitate a solution, and oversees implementation. The children learn the process from the teacher's modeling.

- Facilitating problem solving: The role of the teacher in problem solving and negotiation is to encourage the use of the child's own resources.

Supervision of Children

Consistent supervision of children is key to preventing challenging behavior. Therefore, teaching staff will supervise all infants, toddlers, and two-year-olds by sight and sound at all times. Staff need to be able to hear all infants and toddlers at all times. All infants and toddlers should be easily seen (if not in the direct line of sight, then by looking up or slightly adjusting one's position) by at least one member of the teaching staff. Sight and sound supervision must also be done even when children are sleeping. Staff must be aware of and positioned so they can hear and see any sleeping children, especially when they are actively engaged with children who are awake.

Children who are thirty months of age or older may be momentarily out of sight and sound, as long as the child is back in sight and sound within one minute. Children this age may be supervised by sound only for three minutes on occasion before regaining both sight and sound observation. Children who have had challenging behaviors may need additional supervision.

Addressing Problem Behaviors

On some occasions these methods may not be effective with all children. When this occurs, it is important for the master and supervising teachers to work together to determine whether there is anything in the classroom environment that may be adding to a child's inability to behave appropriately. They may consider the following:

- The physical environment: What is the culture of this particular group of children with their teachers? Do the colors, sounds, and displays represent them? Is the room soft and comfortable? Is it beautiful? Are there obvious places for children to be active or quiet? Is the environment stimulating or overstimulating?

- The emotional environment: Is it possible to meet children's physical needs? Is the room welcoming and inclusive?

- The cultural environment: Is it evident that the classroom values and supports all of the cultures represented? Is there a sense of belonging? "I belong. You belong. They belong."

- The cognitive environment: Does the classroom challenge children and provoke wonder?

- The social environment: Does it meet this group's age range?

The Imagination Children's Center will use three curriculum models in their classrooms as a way to introduce and teach positive social skills to those children who need extra support. These curricula are *Pretend Public Schools Preschool Child Outcomes*, *Second Step*, and *Talking About Touching.* Each of these curricula emphasizes safety and the importance of understanding how someone else feels. They teach children to recognize feelings of others and themselves, to solve their own problems, and to express their anger in nonviolent ways. Each curriculum has the children practice and role play problem situations in order to use them in everyday interactions.

An Individualized Behavior Support Plan is developed for children with persistent, serious, challenging behaviors who are not responding to the above-mentioned guidance techniques. The goal of developing a support plan is to address challenging behaviors and look at productive ways to support children as they learn replacement behaviors. It is the intent that teachers, families, and other professionals work as a team to develop and implement individualized plans that support children's inclusion and success at the center. The steps to developing an Individualized Behavior Support Plan are as follows:

Step 1: Within two weeks of identifying a persistent challenging behavior, the master teacher takes the lead by:

- Creating a communication log to document daily discussions with the family to problem solve together. What is being done at home? Is this something we can do in the center?

- Requesting a medical examination within three weeks to rule out any physiological reason for the behavior.

- During this process, the age-group supervisor and assistant director have begun conducting a minimum of two behavioral observations each week. Observations should create a snapshot of the child's entire day.

- Administering and reviewing social-emotional screening tools, such as ASQ-Social Emotional, to determine whether there are any areas of concern.

Step 2: During regular weekly infant/toddler, transition, or preschool staff meetings, the child's behavior is considered with other team members. Team members brainstorm possible antecedents and suggestions.

During this time, the family will have taken the child for a medical examination. The family meets with the master teacher and supervisor to develop a plan. Families may be asked to journal at home regarding the child's behavior to determine any antecedents in the home environment. The family meets weekly with teaching staff to discuss progress and/or continuing challenges.

The assistant director will contact the behavioral support specialist for input and support. In-depth involvement with the behavioral support specialist will require parental permission.

Step 3: If after three weekly meetings the behavior has not improved, the family meets with the master teacher, supervisor, and assistant director to develop the Individualized Behavioral Support Plan. Issues to be discussed might include:

- hours per week the child is in care. Might reducing the days or hours provide the child with some respite?

- observations made regarding possible triggers for the behavior. It is important that all of the adults in the child's life use the same verbiage when redirecting and/or offering suggestions regarding appropriate behavior.

The Individualized Behavioral Support Plan will continue for one month, during which time regular teacher-family meetings will take place. These meetings may include the master teacher, the supervising teacher, the assistant director, and the child's family.

Step 4: Referrals are made to outside specialists, such as the YMCA, the child's elementary school district office, or the Inclusion and Behavior Consultation Network. The outside specialists will review all previous plans for appropriateness and make suggestions to be added to any plans.

Preparation and Training of Staff on Guidance Policy

All teaching staff will be trained on the child guidance policy during new-employee orientation. In addition, staff will attend regular, ongoing professional development trainings to reinforce and build their knowledge of positive and developmentally appropriate guidance techniques.

Monitoring the Guidance Policy

Child care staff will document evidence of any child who has recurring (two times or more) challenging behaviors. To ensure that the policy is being implemented in practice, site supervisors and master teachers will periodically visit each classroom to evaluate the extent to which the essential features are being implemented. Information from the TAGPEC will be compared with other program data, such as child assessment data, the Classroom Assessment Scoring System, and environmental rating scales, when considering program improvement efforts.

Appendix D: Sample Completed TAGPEC Scoring Form TAGPEC

Program's name: *Learning Is Fun Preschool*

Date filled out: *August 2, 2018*

Completed by: *Matilde Rose*

Role in program: *Director*

Instructions: This checklist is designed to identify different aspects of quality in early care and education guidance policies. This checklist can be completed by a trained program staff member or a specialist in early care and education.

For each question below, please check the response that best describes your program's guidance policy. Check *no* if the policy does not show evidence of addressing the item. Check *emerging* if your policy shows some evidence of addressing the item. Check *yes* if the policy shows clear evidence of addressing the item.

Essential Feature1: Intentional Focus on Teaching Social-Emotional Skills

Early childhood behavior-guidance policies should reflect an instructional, proactive approach to behavior guidance that supports the learning and practice of appropriate prosocial behavior of all children, regardless of individual differences and/or cultural and linguistic background.

Item 1: The policy clearly states that the goal of behavior guidance is to teach social-emotional skills to all children.

☑ Yes   ☐ Emerging   ☐ No

Item 2: The policy clearly describes the role of the teacher in proactively teaching all children social-emotional skills.

☐ Yes   ☑ Emerging   ☐ No

Item 3: The policy clearly describes the role of positive and consistent interactions among teachers and children in promoting positive behavior.

☐ Yes   ☐ Emerging   ☑ No

Item 4: Multiple, evidence-based, developmentally and culturally appropriate strategies are described.

☐ Yes   ☑ Emerging   ☐ No

Essential Feature 2: Developmentally and Culturally Appropriate Learning Environment

Early childhood behavior-guidance policies should describe the importance of a developmentally appropriate learning environment that is predictable, engaging, and relationship based.

Item 5: The policy clearly describes the importance of nurturing and responsive teacher-child relationships as essential to preventing challenging behaviors.

☐ Yes   ☑ Emerging   ☐ No

Item 6: The policy emphasizes the importance of the sufficient and active adult supervision of all children.

☑ Yes   ☐ Emerging   ☐ No

Item 7: The policy describes the need for staff to continuously (at all times) monitor and respond to children's behavior.

☐ Yes   ☐ Emerging   ☑ No

Item 8: The policy clearly describes the use of ecological arrangements, such as classroom environment and materials, as a means for promoting positive, prosocial behavior.

☐ Yes   ☑ Emerging   ☐ No

Item 9: The policy clearly describes the need for a predictable, intentional, and developmentally appropriate daily schedule, including for example small and large group times, carefully planned transitions, and child- and adult-initiated activities.

☐ Yes   ☑ Emerging   ☐ No

Item 10: The policy clearly describes the value of an engaging curriculum that takes a strengths-based view of culture and language as a deterrent to challenging behavior.

☑ Yes   ☐ Emerging   ☐ No

Essential Feature 3: Setting Behavioral Expectations

Early childhood behavior-guidance policies should describe clear and consistent expectations for behavior.

Item 11: The policy has clearly stated program-wide behavioral expectations that are developmentally appropriate and reflect the natural learning abilities typically associated with the age groups of children served. If this item is answered *no,* then items 12–15 also must be answered *no.*

☐ Yes   ☐ Emerging   ☑ No

Item 12: Behavioral expectations are stated positively and emphasize what children can and should do rather than what they cannot do.

☐ Yes   ☐ Emerging   ☑ No

Item 13: Behavioral expectations are designed to promote children's self-regulation, promoting external to internal foci from staff to self.

☐ Yes   ☐ Emerging   ☑ No

Item 14: The policy describes the need for clearly defined rules that are observable and measurable at the classroom level.

☐ Yes   ☐ Emerging   ☑ No

Item 15: The policy describes the need for a connection between program-level behavioral expectations and classroom rules.

☐ Yes   ☐ Emerging   ☑ No

Item 16: The policy clearly describes practices that are unacceptable for use by staff, such as humiliation or depriving meals, snacks, rest, and so on.

☑ Yes   ☐ Emerging   ☐ No

Essential Feature 4: Preventing and Addressing Challenging Behaviors Using a Tiered Model of Intervention

Early childhood behavior-guidance policies should identify primary, secondary, and tertiary preventative and intervention practices for promoting prosocial behavior and reducing challenging behavior in young children.

Item 17: Procedures are in place to screen children for behavioral concerns.

☐ Yes   ☑ Emerging   ☐ No

Item 18: The policy clearly describes the need to understand challenging behavior as children's effort to communicate.

☐ Yes   ☑ Emerging   ☐ No

Item 19: The policy clearly describes primary strategies to teach and reinforce prosocial behaviors in all children. (See Items 1–10).

☑ Yes   ☐ Emerging   ☐ No

Item 20: The policy describes targeted secondary strategies, such as the use of social-skills curricula and intentional small-group instruction, for children who are at risk for problem behaviors.

☐ Yes   ☐ Emerging   ☑ No

Item 21: The policy clearly describes the use of tertiary strategies, such as developing a behavior-support plan, early childhood mental health consultation, and trauma-informed care, for helping children who exhibit chronic and intense problem behaviors.

☐ Yes   ☑ Emerging   ☐ No

Essential Feature 5: Working with Families

Early childhood behavior-guidance policies should reflect the family-centered nature of early childhood education.

Item 22: The policy promotes proactive rather than reactive collaborative relationships as a means of promoting social competence in children.

☑ Yes   ☐ Emerging   ☐ No

Item 23: The policy promotes authentic staff-family collaboration in effectively dealing with challenging behavior, and families are given an opportunity to participate in developing and implementing interventions.

☑Yes   ☐Emerging   ☐No

Item 24: The policy describes the need for obtaining contextually and culturally relevant information, such as at-home sleeping and eating habits, family events, and favorite toys and activities, from families in order to understand children's inappropriate behavior.

☐Yes   ☑Emerging   ☐No

Item 25: The policy promotes embedding individual behavior-support-plan goals and objectives into family-home routines and activities.

☐Yes   ☑Emerging   ☐No

Essential Feature 6: Staff Training and Professional Development

Early childhood behavior-guidance policies should ensure that staff have access to training and technical assistance in implementing policy guidelines and promoting the social competence of young children.

Item 26: The policy describes practices that are in place to ensure that staff understand and can articulate the behavior-guidance policy.

☐Yes   ☑Emerging   ☐No

Item 27: The policy describes a process for ongoing professional-development opportunities to support staff in the use of evidence-based prevention and intervention strategies.

☐Yes   ☑Emerging   ☐No

Item 28: The policy describes the intent of the program to ensure that staff have a strong understanding of culture and diversity and are provided opportunities to engage in self-reflection and ongoing professional development that encourage awareness of implicit and explicit biases that may affect their work with children and families.

☐Yes   ☐Emerging   ☑No

Essential Feature 7: Use of Data for Continuous Improvement

Early childhood behavior-guidance policies should reference the use of a data-collection system by which the relative success or failure of the behavior-guidance policy will be evaluated.

Item 29: Policy-evaluation procedures are in place and clearly describe how the success or failure of the policy will be measured.

☐ Yes ☐ Emerging ☑ No

Item 30: The policy describes how data will be used to engage in continuous improvement to ensure that practices are in line with the intent of the behavior-guidance policy and to ensure fairness and equity for all children.

☐ Yes ☐ Emerging ☑ No

Do you have any concerns about your program's guidance policy?

☐ No ☑ Some ☐ Yes

If you responded *some* or *yes*, please describe your concerns below.

_____

_____

_____

Sample Scored TAGPEC

Steps

Step 1: Calculate score total. *No* = 0 *Emerging* = 1 *Yes* = 2

Step 2: Sum all of the item scores to get a total score.

Step 3: Enter the essential feature scores on the summary section.

Step 4: Enter the total score on the summary section.

Step 5: Higher item scores are strengths.

Summary Section

Essential Feature	Subscale Total Score	Number of Items	Average Score
EF 1: Intentional Teaching Approach Item 1: **2** Item 2: **1** Item 3: **0** Item 4: **1**	**4**	÷ 4	= **1**
EF 2: Developmentally Appropriate Learning Environment Item 5: **1** Item 6: **2** Item 7: **0** Item 8: **1** Item 9: **1** Item 10: **2**	**7**	÷ 6	= **1.17**
EF 3: Setting Behavioral Expectations Item 11: **0** Item 12: **0** Item 13: **0** Item 14: **0** Item 15: **0** Item 16: **2**	**2**	÷ 6	= **0.33**
EF 4: Tiered Model of Intervention Item 17: **1** Item 18: **1** Item 19: **2** Item 20: **0** Item 21: **1**	**5**	÷ 5	= **1**
EF 5: Working with Families Item 22: **2** Item 23: **1** Item 24: **1** Item 25: **1**	**5**	÷ 4	= **1.25**
EF 6: Staff Training and Professional Development Item 26: **1** Item 27: **1** Item 28: **0**	**2**	÷ 3	= **0.67**
EF 7: Data Monitoring and Improvement Item 29: **0** Item 30: **0**	**0**	÷ 2	= **0**
Total: **25**	**25**	÷ 30	= **0.83**

Comments Section

Policy Strengths:

- Clear statement about the importance of social-emotional skills

- Some mention of developmentally appropriate behavior-guidance strategies

- Clear statement about the importance of an engaging curriculum in preventing behavior

- Mentions family collaboration as a part of behavior guidance

- Clearly states what forms of discipline are not acceptable for teachers to use

Policy Areas for Improvement:

- Need a statement about the role of the teacher in proactively teaching social-emotional skills through everyday interactions (Tier 1) and planned instruction (Tier 2)

- Need to add several evidence-based, developmentally appropriate strategies for addressing behavior

- Need program-wide behavioral expectations that are written in simple, positive language and that can be integrated into each classroom

- Add a statement indicating that all staff are trained on how to implement the guidance policy

- Add a statement that explicitly commits to providing the trainings that are needed to fully implement the policy, including addressing implicit bias; using multiple developmentally appropriate behavior-guidance strategies; behavior as communication, behavior screening, and Tier 2 behavior strategies

- Discuss how families' cultural backgrounds and use of guidance at home will be considered during collaboration over problem behavior

Appendix E: TAGPEC Workbook TAGPEC

Worksheet 1: Building a Behavior-Guidance Team

Possible behavior-guidance team members:

- Administrator: Director, Principal, Assistant Director, Assistant Principal

- Office Staff

- Support Staff

- Classroom Teacher

- RTI Coordinator

- Special Education Teacher

- Parents or Guardians

- School Psychologist

- School Counselor or School Social Worker

- Invited Specialists, such as Behavior Coach, Consultants, Foster Youth Services Staff, and Social Worker

Following is a table of team-member roles and responsibilities, to be completed by the coordinator or leader during the first behavior-guidance meeting.

Team Role	Team Responsibilities	Team Members' Names
Coordinator/Leader	• Schedule meetings, communicate meeting dates and agendas to members • Lead meetings: - call meetings to order - introduce team members - review purpose of meeting - summarize problem areas - lead group in problem solving - monitor time - monitor progress	_____
Recorder	• Record problem-solving process • Note contributions made by all team members	_____
Assessor	• Rate school or program's guidance policy using TAGPEC	_____
Data Manager	• Collect data related to behavioral issues, such as behavior incident reports, referrals, behavior-support plans, suspensions and expulsions, and TAGPEC data • Enter new data in file • Maintain data in file	_____
Program or School Team Member	• Share perspective on behavior guidance from the program or school perspective • Collaborate with team to problem solve solutions	_____
Parent Team Member	• Share perspective on behavior guidance from the parent perspective • Collaborate with team to problem solve solutions	_____
Invited Specialists	• Share perspective on behavior guidance from the specialists' perspectives • Collaborate with team to problem solve solutions • Recommend specialists for tier 3 interventions	_____ _____

Tips for Planning the Behavior-Guidance Policy-Improvement Process

Tip 1: Focus the behavior-guidance policy-improvement process solely on improving children's behavior and, by extension, their social, emotional, and academic success.

Tip 2: Allow sufficient meeting time for team members to discuss existing and new behavior-guidance policies.

Tip 3: Allow sufficient meeting time to review the TAGPEC data and to discuss existing guidance policy strengths and areas of need.

Tip 4: Use the data from the TAGPEC scores to guide improvement efforts.

Tip 5: Focus on only a few short- and long-term goals at a time.

Tip 6: Be specific about language your team would like included in the policy.

Worksheet 2: Behavior-Guidance Team Reflection Questions*

This worksheet presents sample questions for reflective thinking during a behavior-guidance policy meeting. The intent is to help staff:

- explore their own discipline experiences,

- develop an understanding of the various perspectives of discipline held by culturally diverse parents and family members,

- identify how culture affects their perspectives on discipline, and

- consider how their views of discipline affect their interactions with children in their work.

These questions should be considered only as a starting point for discussion and further study; they do not represent a comprehensive approach to the issues.

Behavior-Guidance Team Meeting Reflection Questions

1 What do you remember about how your parents or guardians disciplined you growing up? How might your personal background or culture influence your thinking about discipline and child guidance?

2 When do your values and beliefs about discipline conflict with those of families enrolled in your program? How can you discuss these differences in values and beliefs with families in order to benefit the children?

3 What social and emotional skills and behaviors do parents in your program value in their children?

4 What systems or strategies does your program currently have in place to obtain additional information about how discipline is practiced at home and how behavioral interventions are practiced at home?

5 In what ways do the policies and practices of your program reflect information about the families in your program?

6 Reflect on your program's policy statement regarding discipline/guidance. Is there other information that you feel is important that has not yet been included in the definition? Explain.

7 How are families invited by your program to participate in their children's social, emotional, and academic success? Is this reflected in your policy?

8 Does your program have a self-evaluation process for reviewing the effectiveness of your discipline/guidance policy? Please describe.

9 What opportunities do various members of the program and community have to provide input on the guidance policy?

10 What opportunities do program staff have to participate in trainings related to behavior-guidance practices that are embedded in the program's or school's guidance policy?

Sample Behavior-Guidance Commitment Statement

We are committed to providing all children with a strong foundation for social, emotional, and academic success. Our goal is to teach children, through responsive teacher-child interactions, how to develop the skills of self-discipline. We believe that effective child-guidance practices help children to form strong relationships with adults and peers and that these relationships serve as the foundation for development. With support, we believe all children have the potential to grow, discover, play, and learn.

*Adapted from *Multicultural Principles for Head Start Programs Serving Children Ages Birth to Five,* Department of Health and Human Services, Office of Head Start.

Worksheet 3: Behavior-Guidance Document Checklist

Once you have collected all of the available documents on behavior guidance within your program, it is time for you and your team to evaluate each item in relation to your newly developed commitment statement. To do this, we suggest laying the physical documents on a large table and then going through them, one by one, asking the question, "How does this document support our belief and commitment to positive behavior guidance?" (Refer to your completed Worksheet 2 to remind your team of your commitment statement.)

Use the document checklist to list the type of each document in the first column. In the second column, check whether or not the document fulfills an important element of your commitment statement. If it doesn't, then you will want to keep it for reference when you write your final policy draft. Use the third column to make notes about what is working and what is still needed for each of the documents.

One of the most important parts of this process is to determine whether your program is sending a consistent message that reflects your commitment statement. Does the information provided to staff in the staff manual reflect what is in the parent handbook? Is this information consistent with your referral process?

Behavior-Guidance Document Checklist

Type/Name of Document	Does document align with commitment statement? Yes No	Comments What is working? What needs improvement?
_____	_____	_____
_____	_____	_____
_____	_____	_____
_____	_____	_____
_____	_____	_____
_____	_____	_____

Sample Behavior-Guidance Document Checklist

Type/Name of Document	Does Document Align with Commitment Statement? Yes No	Comments What is working? What needs improvement?
Discipline policy, parent handbook	*Yes*	Mission statement aligns with behavior-guidance commitment statement
		Need more details regarding classroom practices
Staff handbook	*No*	Brief information on behavior-guidance approach
		Doesn't include guidance policy mission statement
		Need more details regarding classroom practices
Behavior incident referral form	*No*	States protocol for how discipline is addressed from a safety perspective
		Indicates that parents will be contacted by program when there is a problem or concern
		Need more details about how this form fits into overall behavior-guidance approach
		Need more details about his this form involves families in addressing problem behaviors

Worksheet 4: Behavior-Guidance Policy Action Plan Template

Create a "script" for your improvement effort and support implementation. Develop a work plan for each goal identified through the needs-assessment process. (Feel free to modify the form as needed to fit your unique context.) Distribute copies of the action plan to the members of the collaboration. Keep copies handy to bring to meeting to review and update regularly. You may decide to develop new plans for new phases of your improvement effort.

1 State your goal, and list your action steps.

2 Next, name who will be in charge of each action step.

3 Decide the timeline of each action step; when will each be completed?

4 List the resources you have available, then list the resources you still need. These may be human, financial, political, and so on.

5 List any potential barriers to your action steps. What individuals or organizations might resist?

6 List who will be involved in each action step and how and how often those team members will communicate.

7 Decide how you will show evidence of success—what are your benchmarks?

8 Decide on your evaluation process. List the measures by which you will determine that your goal has been reached.

Goal

_____

_____

_____

Action Steps

Step 1:
_____

Step 2:
_____

Step 3:
_____

Step 4:
_____

Step 5:
_____

Responsibilities

Step 1:

_____

Step 2:

_____

Step 3:

_____

Step 4:

_____

Step 5:

_____

Timeline

Step 1:

_____

Step 2:

_____

Step 3:

_____

Step 4:

_____

Step 5:

_____

Resources Available

Step 1:

_____

Step 2:

_____

Step 3:

_____

Step 4:

_____

Step 5:

_____

Resources Needed

Step 1:

_____

Step 2:

_____

Step 3:

_____

Step 4:

_____

Step 5:

_____

Potential Barriers

Step 1:
_____

Step 2:
_____

Step 3:
_____

Step 4:
_____

Step 5:
_____

Communication

Step 1:
_____

Step 2:
_____

Step 3:
_____

Step 4:
_____

Step 5:
_____

Evidence of Success

_____

_____

_____

_____

_____

Evaluation Process

_____

_____

_____

_____

_____

Resources

Essential Feature 1: Intentional Focus on Teaching Social-Emotional Skills

Books and Articles

Denham, Susanne, Hideko Bassett, Katherine Zinsser, and Todd Wyatt. 2014. "How Preschoolers' Social-Emotional Learning Predicts Their Early School Success: Developing Theory-Promoting, Competency-Based Assessments." *Infant and Child Development* 23(4): 426–454.

Free PDFs

Fox, Lise, and Rochelle Harper Lentini. 2006. '"You Got It!" Teaching Social and Emotional Skills.' *Young Children.* http://challengingbehavior.fmhi.usf.edu/do/resources/documents/yc_article_11_2006.pdf

Websites

Center on the Social and Emotional Foundations for Early Learning, Resources: *What Works* Briefs
http://csefel.vanderbilt.edu/resources/what_works.html

TK California, Social-Emotional Teaching Strategies
http://www.tkcalifornia.org/teaching-tools/social-emotional/teaching-strategies/

Virtual Lab School, Promoting Social-Emotional Development: The Preschool Teacher
https://www.virtuallabschool.org/preschool/social-emotional/lesson-5

Zero to Three, Developing Social-Emotional Skills
https://www.zerotothree.org/resources/series/developing-social-emotional-skills

Essential Feature 2: Developmentally and Culturally Appropriate Learning Environment

Books and Articles

Demby, Gene. 2013. "How Code-Switching Explains the World." Code Switch. NPR. http://www.npr.org/sections/codeswitch/2013/04/08/176064688/how-code-switching-explains-the-world

Derman-Sparks, Louise, and Julie Edwards. 2010. *The Anti-Bias Education for Young Children and Ourselves.* Washington, DC: NAEYC.

Espinosa, Linda. 2014. *Getting It Right for Young Children from Diverse Backgrounds: Applying Research to Improve Practices.* Washington, DC: NAEYC.

Tabors, Patton. 2008. *One Child, Two Languages: A Guide for Early Childhood Educators of Children Learning English as a Second Language.* 2nd edition. Baltimore, MD: Brookes.

Wishard Guerra, Alison, and Sarah Garrity. 2013. "A Cultural Communities and Cultural Practices Approach to Understanding Infant and Toddler Care." In *Infant/Toddler Caregiving: A Guide to Culturally Sensitive Care.* 2nd edition. Sacramento, CA: California Department of Education.

Free PDFs

California Department of Education. 2009. *Preschool English Learners Guide: Principles and Practices to Promote Language, Literacy, and Learning.* Sacramento, CA: Author. http://www.cde.ca.gov/sp/cd/re/documents/psenglearnersed2.pdf

NAEYC. 2009. *Quality Benchmark for Cultural Competence Project.* Washington, DC: Author. https://www.naeyc.org/files/naeyc/file/policy/state/QBCC_Tool.pdf

U. S. Department of Health and Human Services, Administration for Children and Families. 2008. *Revisiting and Updating the Multicultural Principles for Head Start Programs Serving Children Ages Birth to Five.* Washington, DC: Author. https://eclkc.ohs.acf.hhs.gov/hslc/hs/resources/ECLKC_Bookstore/PDFs/Revisiting%20Multicultural%20Principles%20for%20Head%20Start_English.pdf

Websites

Center on the Social Emotional Foundations for Early Learning
http://csefel.vanderbilt.edu/

Head Start Early Childhood Learning and Knowledge Center. Culture and Language.
http://eclkc.ohs.acf.hhs.gov/hslc/tta-system/cultural-linguistic

NAEYC Standing Together against Suspension and Expulsion in Early Childhood
http://www.naeyc.org/suspension-expulsion

Project Implicit, Implicit Association Test (IAT)
https://implicit.harvard.edu/implicit/

Teaching Tolerance
https://www.tolerance.org/

Essential Feature 3: Setting Behavioral Expectations

Books and Articles

McLeod, Bryce, et al. 2017. "Identifying Common Practice Elements to Improve Social, Emotional, and Behavioral Outcomes of Young Children." *Prevention Science* 18(2): 204–213.

Free PDFs

Conroy, Maureen. 2004. *Addressing Challenging Behavior in Early Childhood: Strategies for Teachers and Trainers.* Erlanger, KY: DEC Recommended Practices Training Series. http://challengingbehavior.fmhi.usf.edu/explore/presentation_docs/9.04_addressing_challenging.pdf

Sugai, George. n.d. *School-Wide Positive Behavior Support: School-Wide Expectations—Teaching Matrix Template.* (Word format.) Eugene, OR: Center on Positive Behavioral Interventions and Supports, University of Oregon. www.pbis.org/common/cms/files/NewTeam/manuals/teaching%20matrix.doc

Websites

Edutopia: Behavior Expectations and How to Teach Them
https://www.edutopia.org/blog/behavior-expectations-how-to-teach-them-aaron-hogan

School-Wide Positive Behavioral Interventions and Supports for Beginners
https://www.pbis.org/school/swpbis-for-beginners

Essential Feature 4: Preventing and Addressing Challenging Behaviors Using a Tiered Model of Intervention

Books and Articles

Conroy, Maureen, et al. 2014. "Early Childhood Teachers' Use of Effective Instructional Practices and the Collateral Effects on Young Children's Behavior." *Journal of Positive Behavior Interventions* 16(2): 81–92.

Dougherty, Lea, et al. 2015. "Advances and Directions in Preschool Mental Health Research." *Child Development Perspectives* 9(1): 14–19.

Fox, Lise, and Mary Louise Hemmeter. 2009. "A Program-Wide Model for Supporting Social Emotional Development and Addressing Challenging Behavior in Early Childhood Settings." In *Handbook of Positive Behavior Support.* New York, NY: Springer.

Hemmeter, Mary Louise, Patricia Snyder, Lise Fox, and James Algina. 2016. "Evaluating the Implementation of the 'Pyramid Model for Promoting Social-Emotional Competence' in Early Childhood Classrooms." *Topics in Early Childhood Special Education* 36(3): 133–146.

Free PDFs

Dunlap, Glen, and Lise Fox. 2015. *The Pyramid Model: PBS in Early Childhood Programs and its Relation to School-Wide PBS.* Retrieved from http://challengingbehavior.fmhi.usf.edu/do/resources/documents/PBS%20and%20Pyramid%20Model.pdf

U. S. Department of Health and Human Services and U. S. Department of Education. 2014. *Policy Statement on Expulsion and Suspension Policies in Early Childhood Settings.* Retrieved from http://www.acf.hhs.gov/sites/default/files/ecd/expulsion_suspension_final.pdf

Websites

Association for Positive Behavior Support
http://www.apbs.org/new_apbs/early-childhood.html

Early Childhood PBIS
https://www.pbis.org/community/early-childhood

Technical Assistance Center on Social-Emotional Intervention
https://www.pbis.org/community/early-childhood

Essential Feature 5: Working with Families

Books and Articles

Christenson, Sandra. 2004. "The Family-School Partnership: An Opportunity to Promote the Learning Competence of All Students." *School Psychology Review* 33(1): 83–104.

Cho, Blair K., In-Suk Lee, Su-Je Cho, and Glen Dunlap. 2010. "Positive Behavior Support through Family-School Collaboration for Young Children with Autism." *Topics in Early Childhood Special Education* 31(1): 22–36.

Galuski, Tracy. n.d. "Positive Guidance through the Ages." NAEYC for Families. https://families.naeyc.org/child-development/positive-guidance-through-ages

Jor'dan, Jamilah, Kathy Goetz Wolf, and Anne Douglass. 2012. "Strengthening Families in Illinois: Increasing Family Engagement in Early Childhood Programs." *Young Children* 67(5): 18–23.

Keyser, Janis. 2006. *From Parents to Partners: Building a Family-Centered Early Childhood Education Program.* Washington, DC: NAEYC.

Lucyshyn, Joseph, et al. 2002. "Positive Behavior Support with Families." In *Families and Positive Behavior Support: Addressing Problem Behaviors in Family Contexts.* Baltimore, MD: Brookes.

Websites
Harvard Family Research Project
http://www.hfrp.org/family-involvement/projects

Positive Behavioral Interventions and Supports for Family-Centered PBIS
https://www.pbis.org/community/early-childhood/family-centered-pbis

Essential Feature 6: Staff Training and Professional Development

Books and Articles
Dunlap, Glen, et al. 2000. "Essential Elements of Inservice Training in Positive Behavior Support." *Journal of Positive Behavior Interventions* 2(1): 22–32.

Flannery, Mary Ellen. 2015. "When Implicit Bias Shapes Teacher Expectations." NEA Today. http://neatoday.org/2015/09/09/when-implicit-bias-shapes-teacher-expectations/

Jablon, Judy, Amy Laura Dombro, and Shaun Johnsen. 2016. *Coaching with Powerful Interactions: A Guide for Partnering with Early Childhood Educators.* Washington, DC: NAEYC.

Pianta, Robert, et al. 2014. "Dose-Response Relations between Preschool Teachers' Exposure to Components of Professional Development and Increases in Quality of Their Interactions with Children." *Early Childhood Research Quarterly* 29(4): 499–508.

Free PDFs
Gregory, Anne, et al. 2013. *The Promise of a Teacher Professional Development Program in Reducing the Racial Disparity in Classroom Exclusionary Discipline.* Retrieved from http://gsappweb.rutgers.edu/rts/equityrsch/prodevpdfs/Teacher%20Professional%20Development.pdf

McIntosh, Kent, Beth Hill, and Soraya Coccimiglio. n.d. *Reducing the Effects of Implicit Bias in School Discipline.* Retrieved from https://www.pbis.org/Common/Cms/files/Forum15_Presentations/C4_McIntosh-et-al.pdf

Websites

National Association for the Education of Young Children, Professional Development
https://www.naeyc.org/ecp

U. S. Department of Education, Office of Early Learning, Professional Development
https://www2.ed.gov/programs/eceducator/index.html

Zero to Three, Professional Development
https://www.zerotothree.org/resources/services/professional-development

Essential Feature 7: Use of Data for Continuous Improvement

Books and Articles

Rosenberg, Heidi. 2013. "Embracing the Use of Data for Continuous Program Improvement." Family Involvement Network of Educators (FINE) Newsletter 5(3). http://www.hfrp.org/early-childhood-education/publications-resources/embracing-the-use-of-data-for-continuous-program-improvement

Free PDFs

PBIS World Data Tracking Forms.
Retrieved from http://www.pbisworld.com/data-tracking/

Zweig, Jacqueline, Clare Irwin, Janna Fuccillo Kook, and Josh Cox. 2015. *Data Collection and Use in Early Childhood Programs: Evidence from the Northeast Region.* Report from the National Center for Education Evaluation and Regional Assistance. (REL 2015–084). Washington, DC: U.S. Department of Education, Institute of Education Sciences, National Center for Education Evaluation and Regional Assistance, Regional Educational Laboratory Northeast and Islands. Retrieved from http://files.eric.ed.gov/fulltext/ED555737.pdf

Websites

The National Association of the Education of Young Children: Early Childhood Data
https://www.naeyc.org/policy/statetrends/data

Trauma and Trauma-Informed Care

Free PDFs

The Division for Early Childhood of the Council for Exceptional Children (DEC), NAEYC, and National Head Start Association. 2013. *Frameworks for Response to Intervention in Early Childhood: Description and Implications.* Washington, DC: NAEYC. http://www.naeyc.org/files/naeyc/RTI%20in%20Early%20Childhood.pdf

National Child Traumatic Stress Network. 2008. *Child Trauma Toolkit for Educators.* Rockville, MD: Author.
https://wmich.edu/sites/default/files/attachments/u57/2013/child-trauma-toolkit.pdf

Websites

Collaborative for Academic, Social, and Emotional Learning (CASEL)
http://www.casel.org

Harvard Family Research Project: Family Involvement Projects
http://www.hfrp.org/family-involvement/projects

National Center for Trauma Informed Care
https://www.nasmhpd.org/content/national-center-trauma-informed-care-nctic-0

National Traumatic Stress Network
http://www.nctsn.org

San Diego State University College of Education Teaching and Guidance Policy
Essentials Checklist
http://go.sdsu.edu/education/tagpec/

Positive Behavioral Interventions and Supports (PBIS): School-Wide Positive Behavioral
Interventions and Support for Beginners
https://www.pbis.org/school/swpbis-for-beginners

PBIS, Tier 2 Supports
https://www.pbis.org/school/tier2supports

PBIS, Tier 3 Supports
https://www.pbis.org/school/tier-3-supports

Technical Assistance Center on Social-Emotional Intervention (TACSEI)
http://challengingbehavior.fmhi.usf.edu/communities/families.htm

References

Administration for Youth and Families. 2014. *Child Care and Development Block Grant.* Washington, DC: Author.

Allen, Rosemarie, and Elizabeth Steed. 2016. "Culturally Responsive Pyramid Model Practices: Program-Wide Positive Behavior Support for Young Children." *Topics in Early Childhood Special Education* 36(3): 165–175.

American Psychiatric Association. 2013. *Diagnostic and Statistical Manual of Mental Disorders.* 5th ed. Washington, DC: Author.

Banks, Richard, Jennifer Eberhardt, and Lee Ross. 2006. "Discrimination and Implicit Bias in a Racially Unequal Society." *California Law Review* 94(4): 1169–1190.

Briggs-Gowan, Margaret, et al. 2010. "Exposure to Potentially Traumatic Events in Early Childhood: Differential Links to Emergent Psychopathology." *Journal of Child Psychology and Psychiatry* 51(10): 1132–1140.

Boyd-Franklin, Nancy. 2003. *Black Families in Therapy: Understanding the African American Experience.* 2nd ed. New York: Guilford Press.

Buysse, Virginia, Patricia Wesley, Patricia Snyder, and Pamela Winton. 2006. "Evidence-Based Practice: What Does It Really Mean for the Early Childhood Field?" *Young Exceptional Children* 9(4): 2–11.

Casa de Esperanza. 2003. *Latino Families and Domestic Violence.* Minneapolis, MN: Casa de Esperanza.

Center for Behavioral Health Statistics and Quality. 2015. *2014 National Survey on Drug Use and Health: Methodological Summary and Definitions.* Rockville, MD: Substance Abuse and Mental Health Services Administration. Retrieved from https://www.samhsa.gov/data/sites/default/files/NSDUH-MethodSummDefs2014/NSDUH-MethodSummDefs2014.htm

Chang, Hedy. 2006. *Getting Ready for Quality: The Critical Importance of Developing and Supporting a Skilled, Ethnically and Linguistically Diverse Early Childhood Workforce.* Oakland, CA: California Tomorrow.

Child and Adolescent Health Measurement Initiative. 2013. *2011/2012 National Survey of Children's Health.* HHS Publication: Maternal and Child Health Bureau. Washington, DC: Author.

Ciciolla, Lucia, Keith Crnic, and Emily Gerstein. 2013. "Reciprocity among Maternal Distress, Child Behavior, and Parenting: Transactional Processes and Early Childhood Risk." *Journal of Clinical Child and Adolescent Psychology* 43(5): 751–764.

Coates, Susan, and Theodore Gaensbauer. 2009. "Event Trauma in Early Childhood: Symptoms, Assessment, Intervention." *Child and Adolescent Psychiatric Clinics of North America* 18(3): 611–626.

Colker, Ruth, and Julie Waterstone. 2011. *Special Education Advocacy.* New Providence, NJ: Lexis Nexis.

Conroy, Maureen, Carol Ann Davis, James Fox, and William Brown. 2002. "Functional Assessment of Behavior and Effective Supports for Young Children with Challenging Behavior." *Assessment for Effective Instruction* 27(4): 35–47.

Council for Children with Behavior Disorders. 2002. *School Discipline Policies for Students with Significantly Disruptive Behavior.* Reston, VA: Author. Retrieved from http://www.ccbd.net/documents/jun13_2002.pdf

Crusto, Cindy, et al. 2010. "Posttraumatic Stress among Young Urban Children Exposed to Family Violence and Other Potentially Traumatic Events." *Journal of Traumatic Stress* 23(6): 716–724.

De Young, Alexandra, Justin Kenardy, and Vanessa Cobham. 2011. "Trauma in Early Childhood: A Neglected Population." *Clinical Child and Family Psychology Review* 14(3): 231–250.

Delpit, Lisa. 1995. *Other People's Children: Cultural Conflict in the Classroom.* New York: The New Press.

Derman-Sparks, Louise. 1993. "Revisiting Multicultural Education: What Children Need to Live in a Diverse Society." *Dimensions of Early Childhood* 21(2): 6–10.

Dunlap, Glen, et al. 2003. *Research Synthesis on Effective Intervention Procedures: Executive Summary.* Tampa, FL: University of South Florida, Center for Evidence-Based Practice. Retrieved from: http://www.challengingbehavior.org/explore/publications_docs/research_synthesis.pdf

Dunlap, Glen, Lise Fox, and Mary Louise Hemmeter. 2004. "Program-Wide Approaches for Addressing Children's Challenging Behavior." Symposium Conducted at the Meeting of the National Training Institute on Effective Practices: Supporting Young Children's Social/Emotional Development. Clearwater Beach, FL.

The Education Alliance at Brown University. 2002. *The Diversity Kit: An Introductory Resource for Social Change in Education.* Providence, RI: Brown University.

Edwards, Valerie J., et al. 2005. "The Wide-Ranging Health Consequences of Adverse Childhood Experiences." In *Victimization of Children and Youth: Patterns of Abuse, Response Strategies.* Kingston, NJ: Civic Research Institute.

Felitti, Vincent. 2009. "Adverse Childhood Experiences and Adult Health." *Academic Pediatrics* 9(3): 131–132.

Felitti, Vincent, et al. 1998. "Relationship of Childhood Abuse and Household Dysfunction to Many of the Leading Causes of Death in Adults: The Adverse Childhood Experiences (ACE) Study." *American Journal Preventative Medicine* 14(4): 245–258.

Forgatch, Marion, and Gerald Patterson. 1998. "Behavioral Family Therapy." In *Case Studies in Couple and Family Therapy: Systemic and Cognitive Perspectives.* New York, NY: Guilford Press.

Forness, Steven, et al. 2000. "A Model for Early Detection and Primary Prevention of Emotional or Behavioral Disorders." *Education and Treatment of Children* 23(3): 325–345.

Fox, Lise, et al. 2003. "The Teaching Pyramid: A Model for Supporting Social Competence and Preventing Challenging Behavior in Young Children." *Young Children* 58(4): 48–52.

Fox, Lise, et al. 2011. "Coaching Early Childhood Special Educators to Implement a Comprehensive Model for Promoting Young Children's Social Competence." *Topics in Early Childhood Special Education* 31(3): 178–192.

García Coll, Cynthia, et al. 1996. "An Integrative Model for the Study of Developmental Competencies in Minority Children." *Child Development* 67(5): 1891–1914.

Garnes, Lori, and Ronda Menlove. 2003. "School-Wide Discipline Practices: A Look at the Effectiveness of Common Practices." Paper presented at Rural Survival: 23rd Annual Conference of the American Council on Rural Special Education, Salt Lake City, UT.

Garrity, Sarah, Alyson Shapiro, Sascha Longstreth, and J. Bailey. 2017. "Socializing Children to Be *Bien Educado:* The Role of Culture on Early Childhood Educator Beliefs about Discipline, Teaching, and Children." Proceedings from the Biennial Meeting of the Society for Research on Child Development, Austin, TX.

Gay, Geneva. 2010. *Culturally Responsive Teaching: Theory, Research, and Practice.* 2nd edition. New York: Teachers College Press.

Gilliam, Walter, et al. 2016. "Do Early Educators' Implicit Biases Regarding Sex and Race Relate to Behavior Expectations and Recommendations of Preschool Expulsions and Suspensions?" New Haven, CT: Yale University, Edward Zigler Center in Child Development and Social Policy. http://ziglercenter.yale.edu/publications/Preschool%20Implicit%20 Bias%20Policy%20Brief_final_9_26_276766_5379.pdf

Goodman, Rachael, David Miller, and Cirecie West-Olatunji. 2012. "Traumatic Stress, Socioeconomic Status, and Academic Achievement among Primary School Students." *Psychological Trauma: Theory, Research, Practice, and Policy* 4(3): 252–259.

Gonzalez-Mena, Janet. 2001. "Cross-Cultural Infant Care and Issues of Equity and Social Justice." *Contemporary Issues in Early Childhood* 2(3): 368–371.

Gonzalez-Mena, Janet. 2008. *Diversity in Early Care and Education: Honoring Differences.* New York: McGraw-Hill.

Grisham-Brown, Jennifer, Mary Louise Hemmeter, and Kristi Pretti-Frontczak. 2005. *Blended Practices for Teaching Young Children in Inclusive Settings.* Baltimore, MD: Paul H. Brookes.

Gutierrez, Kris, and Barbara Rogoff. 2003. "Cultural Ways of Learning: Individual Traits or Repertoires of Practice." *Educational Researcher* 32(19): 19–25.

Hale, Janice. 1983. "Black Children: Their Roots, Culture, and Learning Styles." In *Understanding the Multicultural Experience in Early Childhood Education.* Washington, DC: NAEYC.

Hale, Janice. 2001. *Learning while Black: Creating Educational Excellence for African American Children.* Baltimore, MD: Johns Hopkins University Press.

Heath, Shirley. 1983. *Ways with Words: Language, Life, and Work in Communities and Classrooms.* Cambridge, UK: Cambridge University Press.

Institute of Medicine (IOM) and National Research Council (NRC). 2012. *The Early Childhood Care and Education Workforce: Challenges and Opportunities: A Workshop Report.* Washington, DC: The National Academies Press.

Kagan, Sharon Lynn, Kristie Kauerz, and Kate Tarrant. 2007. *The Early Care and Education Teaching Workforce at the Fulcrum: An Agenda for Reform.* New York, NY: Teachers College Press.

Kaiser, Barbara, and Judy Rasminsky. 2011. *Challenging Behavior in Young Children: Understanding, Preventing, and Responding Effectively.* 3rd edition. New York, NY: Pearson.

Kochman, Thomas. 1985. "Black American Speech Events and a Language Program for the Classroom." In *Functions of Language in the Classroom.* Prospect Heights, IL: Waveland.

Lieberman, Alicia, and Kathleen Knorr. 2007. "The Impact of Trauma: A Developmental Framework for Infancy and Early Childhood." *Psychiatric Annals* 37(6): 416–422.

Leithwood, Kenneth, et al. 2006. *Seven Strong Claims about Successful School Leadership.* Nottingham, UK: National College for School Leadership. http://dera.ioe.ac.uk/6967/1/download%3Fid%3D17387%26filename%3Dseven-claims-about-successful-school-leadership.pdf

Lewis, Timothy, and George Sugai. 1999. "Effective Behavior Support: A Systems Approach to Proactive School-Wide Management." *Focus on Exceptional Children* 31(6): 1–24.

Lindsey, Randall, Stephanie Graham, Chris Westphal Jr., and Cynthia Jew. 2007. *Culturally Proficient Inquiry: A Lens for Identifying and Examining Educational Gaps.* Thousand Oaks, CA: Corwin.

McEvoy, Alan, and Robert Welker. 2000. "Antisocial Behavior, Academic Failure, and School Climate: A Critical Review." *Journal of Emotional and Behavioral Disorders* 8(3):130–140.

McIntosh, Kent, Aaron Barnes, Bert Eliason, and Kelsey Morris. 2014. *Using Discipline Data within SWPBIS to Identify and Address Disproportionality: A Guide for School Teams.* Eugene, OR: OSEP Technical Assistance Center on Positive Behavioral Interventions and Supports, University of Oregon. https://www.pbis.org/Common/Cms/files/pbisresources/ PBIS_Disproportionality_Data_Guidebook.pdf

McLoyd, Vonnie, Nancy Hill, and Kenneth Dodge, eds. 2005. *African American Family Life: Ecological and Cultural Diversity.* New York: Guilford Press.

Meier, Kenneth, Joseph Stewart, Jr., and Robert England. 1989. *Race, Class and Education: The Politics of Second-Generation Discrimination.* Madison, WI: University of Wisconsin Press.

Milner, Richard. 2011. "Culturally Relevant Pedagogy in a Diverse Urban Classroom." *Urban Review* 43(1): 66–89.

Mitgang, Lee. 2012. *The Making of the Principal: Five Lessons in Leadership Training.* New York: The Wallace Foundation. www.wallacefoundation.org/knowledge-center/ school-leadership/effective-principal-leadership/Documents/The-Making -of-the-Principal- Five-Lessons-in-Leadership-Training.pdf

Moldenhauer-Salazar, Jay. 2000. "Visions and Missions: A Case Study of Organizational Change and Diversity in Higher Education." *Dissertation Abstracts International: Section B. Sciences and Engineering* 61(2): 1120.

Molinsky, Andrew. 2007. "Cross-Cultural Code-Switching: The Psychological Challenges of Adapting Behavior in Foreign Cultural Interactions." *Academy of Management Review* 32(2): 622–640.

Monk, Catherine, Julie Spicer, and Frances Champagne. 2012. "Linking Prenatal Maternal Adversity to Developmental Outcomes in Infants: The Role of Epigenetic Pathways." *Developmental Psychopathology* 24(4): 1361–1376.

Monroe, Carla. 2009. "Teachers Closing the Discipline Gap in an Urban Middle School." *Urban Education* 44(3): 322–347.

NAEYC. 1995. *Responding to Linguistic and Cultural Diversity: Recommendations for Effective Early Childhood Education.* Position Statement. Washington, DC: Author.

NAEYC et al. 2016. *Standing Together against Suspension and Expulsion in Early Childhood.* Washington, DC: Author.

National Center for Juvenile Justice. 2014. *Juvenile Offenders and Victims: 2014 National Report.* Pittsburgh, PA: National Center for Juvenile Justice.

National Research Council (NRC) and Institute of Medicine (IOM). 2009. *Preventing Mental, Emotional, and Behavioral Disorders Among Young People: Progress and Possibilities.* Committee on the Prevention of Mental Disorders and Substance Abuse Among Children, Youth and Young Adults: Research Advances and Promising Interventions. Washington, DC: The National Academies Press.

Perry, Bruce D. 2013. *Bonding and Attachment in Maltreated Children: Consequences of Emotional Neglect in Childhood.* Houston, TX: Child Trauma Academy. https://childtrauma.org/wp-content/uploads/2013/11/Bonding_13.pdf

Perry, Bruce. 2014. "The Neurosequential Model of Therapeutics: Application of a Developmentally Sensitive and Neurobiology-Informed Approach to Clinical Problem Solving in Maltreated Children." In *Infant and Early Childhood Mental Health: Core Concepts and Clinical Practice.* Arlington, VA: American Psychiatric Publishing.

Powell, Diane, Dean Fixsen, and Glen Dunlap. 2003. *Pathways to Service Utilization: A Synthesis of Evidence Relevant to Young Children with Challenging Behavior.* Tampa, FL: University of South Florida, Center for Evidence-Based Practice: Young Children with Challenging Behavior.

Rashid, Hakim. 2009. "From Brilliant Baby to Child Placed at Risk: The Perilous Path of African American Boys in Early Childhood Education. *The Journal of Negro Education* 78(3): 347–358.

Rogers, Carl. 1961. *On Becoming a Person: A Therapist's View of Psychotherapy.* London, UK: Constable.

Rothstein-Fisch, Carrie, et al. 2010. "Uncovering the Role of Culture in Learning, Development, and Education." In *Innovations in Educational Psychology: Perspectives on Learning, Teaching, and Human Development.* New York: Springer.

Sameroff, Arnold, and Michael MacKenzie. 2003. "Research Strategies for Capturing Transactional Models of Development: The Limits of the Possible." *Development and Psychopathology* 15(3): 613–640.

Schweinhart, Lawrence, et al. 2005. *Lifetime Effects: The High-Scope Perry Preschool Study through Age 40.* Ypsilanti, MI: High Scope Press.

Shade, Barbara, and Patricia Edwards. 1987. "Ecological Correlates of the Educative Style of Afro-American Children." *The Journal of Negro Education* 56(1): 88–99.

Shade, Barbara, Cynthia Kelly, and Mary Oberg. 1997. *Creating Culturally Responsive Classrooms.* Washington, D.C.: American Psychological Association.

Sheldon, Stephen, and Joyce Epstein. 2002. "Improving Student Behavior and School Discipline with Family and Community Involvement." *Education and Urban Society* 35(1): 4–26.

Sickmund, Melissa, and Charles Puzzanchera, eds. 2014. *Juvenile Offenders and Victims: 2014 National Report.* Pittsburgh, PA: National Center for Juvenile Justice.

Skiba, Russell, Robert Michael, Abra Carroll Nardo, and Reece Peterson. 2002. "The Color of Discipline: Sources of Racial and Gender Disproportionality in School Punishment." *The Urban Review* 34(4): 317–342.

Stepp, Stephanie, et al. 2012. "Children of Mothers with Borderline Personality Disorder: Identifying Parenting Behaviors as Potential Targets for Intervention." *Personality Disorders: Theory, Research, and Treatment* 3(1): 76–91.

Strain, Phillip, and Gail Joseph. 2004. "A Not So Good Job with 'Good Job': A Response to Kohn 2001." *Journal of Positive Behavior Interventions* 6(1): 55–59.

Sugai, George, and Robert Horner. 2002. "The Evolution of Discipline Practices: School-Wide Positive Behavior Supports." *Child and Family Behavior Therapy* 24(1–2): 23–50.

Togut, Torin. 2011. "The Gestalt of the School-to-Prison Pipeline: The Duality of Overrepresentation of Minorities in Special Education and Racial Disparity in School Discipline on Minorities." *Journal of Gender, Social Policy, and the Law* 20(1): 163–181.

Turnbull, Ann, Rutherford Turnbull, Elizabeth Erwin, and Leslie Soodak. 2006. *Families, Professionals, and Exceptionality: Positive Outcomes through Partnership and Trust.* 5th edition. Upper Saddle River, NJ: Pearson.

Turner, Heather, et al. 2012. "Family Context, Victimization, and Child Trauma Symptoms: Variations in Safe, Stable, and Nurturing Relationships during Early and Middle Childhood." *American Journal of Orthopsychiatry* 82(2): 209–219.

U.S. Department of Education. 2014. *Guiding Principles: A Resource Guide for Improving School Climate and Discipline.* Washington, DC: Author.

U.S. Department of Education, Office for Civil Rights. 2014. *Civil Rights Data Collection: Data Snapshot: Early Childhood Education.* Issue Brief No. 2. Washington, DC: U.S. Department of Education.

U.S. Department of Health and Human Services, Office of Head Start, Administration for Children and Families. 2016. *Head Start Program Performance Standards.* Washington, DC: Office of Head Start, Administration for Children and Families.

U.S. Department of Health and Human Services and U.S. Department of Education. 2014. *Policy Statement on Expulsion and Suspension Policies in Early Childhood Settings.* Washington, DC: U.S. Department of Health and Human Services.

Vincent, Claudia, et al. 2011. "Toward a Conceptual Integration of Cultural Responsiveness and Schoolwide Positive Behavior Support." *Journal of Positive Behavior Interventions* 13(4): 219–229.

Vygotsky, Lev. 1962. *Thought and Language.* Cambridge, MA: MIT Press.

Vygotsky, Lev. 1981. "The Genesis of Higher Mental Functions: The Concept of Activity in Soviet Psychology." In *The Concept of Activity in Soviet Psychology.* Armonk, NY: M E Sharpe.

Walsh, Froma, ed. 2009. *Spiritual Resources in Family Therapy.* 2nd ed. New York: Guilford Press.

Washburn, Sandra, Leonard Burrello, and Stephen Buckmann. 2001. *School-Wide Behavioral Support: A Resource Guide for Facilitators.* Bloomington, IN: Indiana University, Forum on Education.

Webster-Stratton, Carolyn, Jamila Reid, and Mary Hammond. 2001. "Treating Children with Early-Onset Conduct Problems: Intervention Outcomes for Parent, Child, and Teacher Training." *Journal of Clinical Child and Adolescent Psychology* 33(1): 105–124.

Weinstein, Carol, Saundra Tomlinson-Clarke, and Mary Curran. 2004. "Toward a Conception of Culturally Responsive Classroom Management." *Journal of Teacher Education* 55(1): 25–38.

Zeanah, Charles Jr., and Paula Zeanah. 2009. "The Scope of Infant Mental Health." In *Handbook of Infant Mental Health.* 3rd ed. New York, NY: Guilford Press.

Zero to Three. 2005. *Diagnostic Classification of Mental Health and Developmental Disorders of Infancy and Early Childhood.* Rev. ed. (DC: 0–3R). Washington, DC: Zeroto Three.

Zindler, Patricia, Anne Hogan, and Mimi Graham. 2010. *Addressing the Unique and Trauma-Related Needs of Young Children.* Florida State University Center for Prevention and Early Intervention Policy: Tallahassee, FL.

Zins, Joseph, Michelle Bloodworth, Roger Weissberg, and Herbert Walberg. 2004. "The Scientific Base Linking Social and Emotional Learning to School Success." In *Building Academic Success on Social and Emotional Learning: What Does the Research Say?* New York, NY: Teachers College Press.

Index

A

ABCs of behavior analysis, 23
Abuse, 22, 84–85, 89–93, 97
Acculturation, 36–37
Adaptation, 37
Adapting materials, 50
Addiction, 25
Adult-child relationships, 88–89
Adverse childhood experiences, 85–87
Age, 24–26
Aggression, 6, 16, 84, 93, 98–99
Alcoholism, 85
American Psychiatric Association, 93
Analgesia, 89
Anesthesia, 90
Anxiety, 89, 98
Assembling a team, 74–75
Assessment, 78–79
Assimilation, 37
Attachment, 19–21, 88–89
Attention seeking, 21, 23, 25
Attention-deficit/hyperactivity disorder, 93, 96, 98
Avoidance, 99

B

Behavior, 20–24, 27, 41–42, 91–92, 97
Behavioral-guidance policies, 1, 5–13
　　addressing implicit bias, 45
　　behavior is communication, 16, 20–24
　　developmentally/culturally appropriate environment, 47, 50–51
　　essential features, 47–57
　　evaluating, 56–57
　　five steps, 71, 74–79
　　humanistic approach, 15–27, 75
　　implicit bias, 16, 26–27
　　improving with TAGPEC, 71–79
　　individual differences, 16, 24–26
　　intentional focus, 47–50, 60–63
　　monitoring, 79
　　reframing views of challenging behaviors, 27
　　relational, 16, 18–20
　　role of leadership, 72–74
　　sample, 114–118
　　setting behavioral expectations, 47, 51–52
　　staff training/development, 47, 55–56
　　teacher's role, 16–18
　　tiered model of intervention, 47, 52–54
　　use of data, 47, 56–57
　　working with families, 47, 54–55
Biculturalism, 37
Bilingual educational services, 30
Biting, 6, 21
Brainstorming, 49
Bullying, 84

C

California Department of Education, 138
Casa de Esperanza, 37
Center for Behavioral Health Statistics and Quality, 100
Center on the Developing Child at Harvard University, 87, 89
Center on the Social and Emotional Foundations for Early Learning, 10, 43
Centers for Disease Control and Prevention, 85
Challenging behaviors, 1, 6, 12–13, 17–18, 20–24, 27, 41–42, 47, 51–54, 84, 97
Child Care and Development Fund policy initiatives, 11
Children of color, 6–7, 26–27, 31–39, 44–45, 88
Children with disabilities, 6–7, 26–27
Choices, 18, 63
Code switching, 36–39
Collaboration, 72–73
Collecting documents, 76–77
Commitment, 72–73
Conflict-solving skills, 17, 61, 68
Continuous improvement, 56–57
Corporal punishment, 34
Council for Children with Behavior Disorders, 51, 55
Council for Exceptional Children, 81
Creativity, 72–74
Criminal behavior, 6, 84
Critical-thinking skills, 7, 90–91, 94
Cultural influences, 2, 6–7, 24–26
Culturally appropriate environment, 13, 47, 50–51, 63, 137–138